The
Single Girl's
Survival
Guide

The Single Girl's Survival Guide

Secrets for Today's Savvy, Sexy, and Independent Woman

Imogen Lloyd Webber

Skyhorse Publishing

THE SINGLE GIRL'S SURVIVAL GUIDE

Skyhorse Publishing books may be purchased in bulk at special discounts for sales promotion, corporate gifts, fund-raising, or educational purposes. Special editions can also be created to specifications. For details, contact the Special Sales Department, Skyhorse Publishing, 307 West 36th Street, 11th Floor, New York, NY 10018 or info@skyhorsepublishing.com.

Skyhorse® and Skyhorse Publishing® are registered trademarks of Skyhorse Publishing, Inc.®, a Delaware corporation.

Visit our website at www.skyhorsepublishing.com.

10 9 8 7 6 5 4 3 2 1

Library of Congress Cataloging-in-Publication Data is available on file.

Cover design by Jane Sheppard
Cover illustration by iStockphoto

Print ISBN: 978-1-5107-3125-7

Printed in China

For my lovely Mum

CONTENTS

A Single Girl's Survival Guide Glossary

AG: Attached Girl.

ALL TEXT NO TROUSERS: Phrase used to describe a man who texts on a regular basis suggesting you should meet up, but never actually comes up with a date (see also **Clit Teaser**).

AS: Accidental Sex, an **SG's** version of the one-night stand. Only in exceptional circumstances will an **SG** have had a premeditated intention for an encounter to unfold in so unclothed a way as it did, or be under the impression there will be no repeat performances.

BIG DUVET: Time spent in one's own abode under one's very own duvet.

BF: Best Friend. Even more precious to you than your shoe collection.

BUNBURY: From Oscar Wilde's *The Importance of Being Earnest*; an imaginary friend with a very real role in getting an **SG** out of things she would rather not do.

CABBAGE: A cab/taxi; somewhere the in-demand **SG** aims to spend a significant proportion of her time, for then her heels can be high *and* she has a chance of making almost all her engagements.

CLIT TEASER: An **Object/Distraction** who flirts, but does not follow through.

CL: Conversation List. A thought process or written list prepared for any type of discussion, with a number of questions for you to ask and replies to inquiries likely to be aimed in your direction.

DISTRACTION: A male (or even female) an **SG** has her eye on for non-platonic affairs (see also **Object**).

DO DINNER OFF THE MIRROR (VERB): To eschew food for **hoovering** cocaine.

EXPLOITATION: Exploitation of skills, knowledge, or items obtained from your ex-boyfriends to improve your lifestyle.

FYI (VERB): From the abbreviation "For Your Information". To let someone know something of pertinence.

GBF: Gay Best Friend.

GENUINE GIRLFRIEND: A female friend whom an **SG** can confide in with complete confidence and who absolutely always abides by the "girl's code" of behavior, never **kissing** any of said **SG's** exes.

GIRL PLAYMATE: A female friend who is fantastic to have fun with, but is not necessarily a suitable person to divulge your deepest, darkest secrets to.

HOOVER (VERB): To snort cocaine.

HORRORSCOPES: Horoscopes. To be consulted sparingly and with a spoonful of salt.

IPOD ICEBREAKER: A textbook conversation-creating tactic, where a person asks another what the most embarrassing song on his/her iPod is, then reveals theirs.

IN HARM'S WAY: To put yourself in with a chance of attaining something you desire, most often a new **Distraction/Object** or job.

JOINER: A sanctimonious soul who enjoys organized group activities. If said activities take place outside, **Joiners** will be keen they go ahead whatever the weather.

KISS (VERB): A euphemism which covers all exchange of bodily fluids between an **SG** and a **Distraction/Object**, i.e., from literally just kissing someone to full-blown sex.

KISS AND CUDDLE (VERB): Full-blown sex.

METROSEXUAL: A male who spends a vast proportion of his disposable income on his grooming and lifestyle.

NFI (VERB): To Not F**king Invite someone to an event; the aim of the game is to be FI'd as much as possible.

OBJECT: As in Object of Affection; a male (or female) an **SG** has her eye on for non-platonic affairs (see also **Distraction**).

PB: Platonic Boyfriend. A male friend of the **SG** whom she does not **kiss**; the "Boy" version of the **Girl Playmate**.

PLAY (VERB): The adult version of children's "play." To have fun; may encompass **kissing**.

PMDL: A Promise Much, Deliver Little boy. PMDLs are a selection of scoundrels who bruise egos or even break hearts.

PRE-BOUND (VERB): To find a new job/relationship before ditching the old one.

PULL THE RIPCORD (VERB): To decide it is time to exit a gathering. Your **Wingman** may occasionally have to pull your ripcord for you if you have been the life and soul of the party a little too long and have suddenly come over all emotional.

RADIO CONTACT: Contact with friends via cell phone.

RETROSEXUAL: A male who spends the smallest proportion possible of his disposable income on grooming and lifestyle, preferring the caveman approach.

SG: The Single Girl, our heroine.

S&MBF: Straight and Male Best Friend.

SOCIAL HAND GRENADE: A person who will cause chaos whatever the social setting. Best for an **SG** not to select as a **Wingman**, unless she is mischief-making.

SQUEAKY: A small, stupid female who is a man's woman, rather than a girly girl. Will blank an **SG** if she has a **Distraction** she can flirt with in the vicinity.

WINGMAN: The person from an **SG's** friends whom she chooses to accompany her on events/nights out, etc. Identity will alter, depending on function.

INTRODUCTION

*I*T IS A truth which should be universally acknowledged that a single girl can be in possession of the most wonderful life. No longer is the **Single Girl (SG)** one of Jane Austen's husband hunters, or simply a "spinster;" instead, think Bridget Jones and Carrie Bradshaw. Single women are allowing themselves to be celebrated—but to a point. Both Bridget and Carrie only reach fulfillment when they ride off into the sunset with Mr. Darcy and Mr. Big.

"One day your prince will come" goes the saying: but what if your knight-in-shining-Armani's GPS has sent him up a one-way street? Is the SG to sit and pine? Or waste her time desperately seeking (stalking?) a man, which is enough to make any male specimen sprint in the opposite direction—especially if he hears her biological clock ticking like Peter Pan's crocodile? When a relationship is right, it is wondrous. But when it's not, what is the point? You can be lonelier in the wrong relationship than you can ever be when you are single. Being attached is fun, but as an SG you have so many delicious possibilities to explore. You may not be unattached forever—so take advantage of the single lifestyle while you can. Seize the day.

I have been single for the best part of the last ten years, almost all my adult life. I've dated and had relationships in that time, but I've been single through most of it. (I remain so as I write this.) I love men—there is nothing so heady and fabulous as being in lust, or even love—but I've found it a challenge to meet worthy ones. I admit I am fussy, but I'm also fussy about my handbags, and I like a male to last longer on my arm than a purse does. When it comes to boyfriends, you are allowed to be careful.

Being without a man is really not the life or death crisis it's often made out to be; I can't remember the last time a friend made me cry, but I could tell you exactly when a man did. Moreover, I have witnessed the destructiveness of divorce: choosing to be with someone, maybe making a life together, is a decision that has to be right. And if no knight-in-almost-shining-armor comes (no relationship is perfect, but it is important to have a half-decent starting point), I will be OK.

A simple truth. There is, funnily enough, a direct link between the person you breed with and whether those children turn out to be happy, well-adjusted souls or not. Detractors of women leaving it later to have babies neglect to admit that, half the time, these SGs just didn't meet someone they were confident would be a good father. They should be praised for saving society, not screwing it up (and for propping up the shoe industry with their disposable income).

I have not always felt this way: the stresses and strains of modern life once overwhelmed this SG. But when everything went wrong, I recovered from my meltdown by managing the parts—and people—of my world that I could in small steps, and in time I found myself not just running but sprinting through my days again. In my decade of "research" for this book, I have had the most extraordinary experiences and heard (even featured in) the most scandalous tales, many of which I've referred to. I've withheld the names to protect the guilty, but their actions will illustrate how to put a sparkle into your SG smile.

This book is not about how to find a man. Tongue embedded firmly in cheek, it is about how to survive as a modern SG, steering a safe passage through the stormy waters of your world, to limit the seasickness and even enjoy the trip. Of course, the side effect of successfully managing your life is that your innate air of confidence will attract at least one male who will want to play to your tune (although they might need a little encouragement/manipulation to get the opening notes right).

This expedition is a comprehensive one. We start with managing your working life: from handling your boss and obnoxious (especially on Valentine's Day) colleagues, to survival skills for work functions, including the Office Christmas Party. Everything you need to know to be mistress of the workplace is here.

As SGs, we have the advantage of being able to devote more time to the body beautiful: from medicals to manicures, this is your moment to focus on you (there's even a chapter to show you exactly how to go about it). To attain your inner body beautiful, you will be doing battle with unsympathetic doctors, gynecologists, and a myriad of alternative-health gurus. Then there is the creation of the outer body beautiful—from diet and gym etiquette to shopping. When you're single, you have the benefit of never being made to feel that clothes and shoes are a luxury, or that there are more necessary purchases to be made; *they* are a necessity, part of the armor of modern life.

The way you live your life is your call. Home is your domain: If you want, you can take pride in it and perfectly feng shui your pad without fear of a man's smelly sneakers or a child's noisy plastic playthings destroying your vibe. You can choose a prime, urban location and live in a place so small a cat couldn't reside, never mind swing with you in, or find somewhere that comfortably contains your entire collection of footwear, but which you can neither get a taxi from nor to. Whether buying or renting, real estate agents need to be played (sorry, managed) and so are up for scrutiny. And to share or not to share . . . that is the roommate question.

Family, like everything else, also needs to be managed. This is true whatever one's age or marital status, but especially for a single woman with ovaries still grumbling once a month. Be prepared, in good Girl Guide style, for any curve balls they throw at you and, most importantly, for Festive Season Survival.

Friends, which are the family you get to pick, are essential. They're your support network when you are down, your playmates when you want to have fun—but they too need to be managed: found, kept, and, in some instances, dropped. It's crucial to have certain types of friends: the **Genuine Girlfriends** and perhaps even a **Best Friend (BF)**; a **Gay Best Friend (GBF)** if you can find one; **Platonic Boyfriends (PBs),** and, of course, your **Bunbury**. Bunbury, a term coined by Oscar Wilde in *The Importance of Being Earnest*, is an imaginary friend who can provide a convenient excuse or example for almost anything.

From your friends you'll learn how to choose the right **Wingman** (aka your "plus one" or your "Walker") for the right occasion; no need to fly solo just because you're single. Being out having fun is something that we SGs can do better and more often than anyone; we are not beholden to another's diary and body clock. But we also have standards—as SGs we *know* what a good party is. Preparation is key in choosing whether to attend an occasion, so you must be aware of the dangers of social situations, such as going to a restaurant with a ridiculing relative, the Couply Dinner Party, the "Hen Night," the

Wedding, and New Year's Eve; and the measures that can be taken to minimize the damage in each case.

Attending these events will by default put you **in harm's way**—that is, in contact with the male of the species. It's only natural that you will come across one who is attracted to the happy-in-herself you. There is nothing wrong with having a **Distraction**, an **Object of Affection (Object)**, as long as he makes you smile. There is a socially acceptable age range for your Distraction (even a mathematical formula) and a mélange of advantages and disadvantages to the younger man, the older man, the rich man, the student, the bisexual . . .

The early stages of a flirtation resemble what a manager of a sporting team goes through when selecting new players. You need a game plan to successfully negotiate modern-day communication. Used correctly, mobiles and computers can reel in the prey, but *he-mail* banter can be tricky, and mobile phones used at inappropriate times are more akin to unexploded hand grenades.

Dates are littered with potential obstacles, from dinners with chopsticks and garlic noodles to who holds the popcorn at the movies. And, of course, **"kissing"** (a polite euphemism for anything from kissing to full-blown sex) is one messy, complicated, yet delicious minefield. There's also the one-night stand, aka **Accidental Sex (AS),** the walk of shame, the positively virginal fifth-date rule, and the naughty territory of S&M, sex toys, and so on . . . If you are happy to go that way, fine; escape routes are offered here if you are not.

So are you single? Ultimately, it's all about you. You are whole, not half. Don't compromise your world for someone who doesn't appreciate what a catch you are. You have friends who will actually help you assemble those bookshelves, rather than just look at them in pieces, and a vibrator that will dependably give you an orgasm, not fall asleep halfway through because of one beer too many (always keep spare batteries!). You can have the most amazing existence as an SG. This *Single Girl's Survival Guide* says hold on tight and be prepared for the ride of your life.

CHAPTER 1

Work Management

THE FIRST CRUCIAL steppingstone to the **SG**'s conquest of the world—whether debt-ridden graduate or lottery winner—is employment. When I was in my early 20s, I fell apart. Career, health, home, and men; everything went wrong at once. How did I get out of it? The first move was finding a job (albeit a hideous one), which gave me time to find a better mode of employment, allayed some of my family's more vocal concerns, and helped me deal with a misdiagnosis courtesy of my doctors. Slowly, everything else began to fall into place.

A job, even if it's just a stopgap, makes you feel better about yourself. Packing your day with purpose also prevents you from overanalyzing your life. Some self-awareness and analysis is a good thing; too much leads you to endlessly pondering your life instead of living it. Throwing yourself into work is a proven tactic to take your mind off emotional malaise. A girlfriend of mine who worked for her father got ditched by her long-term boyfriend; her dad wisely tripled her workload. This got her through the shell shock stage (normally the first few days), when you have to cope with the very real sense of loss caused by the simple lack of the ex's physical presence. My friend was literally too busy to cry; very soon, she was loving the bachelorette lifestyle. If you are frantically managing the mundane, when you do address weightier issues, it tends to be with a calmer, more balanced perspective. When my friend finally found the time to consider the split, she decided, quite rationally, it had been a lucky escape not to be married at 25.

Employment not only satisfies the innate necessity humans have to fill their days; it also brings income. You get to move out of your parents' home, buy shoes, and to **play** (have fun). Of course, you still have to part with the chunk of cash that goes to that nasty taxman and to mean financial institutions that use words like "debt" and "overdue." However, what remains is all for you. There is no need to justify to a protesting partner the purchase of an accessory rather than an ironing board, or a manicure instead of some new paint. You are not contributing toward football season tickets (unless they are for you).

There may well be a time, namely the rest of your life, to berate yourself for not lavishing appropriate time or cash on your partner or children (or both). Women excel at guilt, so celebrate your moment now. Take pleasure from knowing you're probably never going to feel less at fault, look more glamorous, or have the possibility to play more than at this stage of your life.

• **FINDING A JOB** •

Every job can be boring sometimes. If yours is exceptionally dull, view it merely as a launching pad to a better one. In the meantime, hang in there. Unlike relationships, where it's always best to leave if you are in an unhappy dead end, perseverance pays off with work. While finding a new boyfriend when still with the old is never clever (and has even less chance of success than a rebound relationship), it's perfectly acceptable—even advisable—to take such an approach in the workplace. It's easier to find a new job, to **pre-bound** into a better one, when you are employed elsewhere.

When deciding what you want to do, ask your most honest friends for a reality check. Even if your particular brand of freak value could make you a reality-show winner, it's no guarantee of any sort of career longevity. Reach for the stars, but ones that you have a realistic chance of attaining—if you really can sing, then pull out the stops to make the next American Idol audition. Just make sure you have a backup plan with more weight than a Rachel Zoe client.

Once you have decided on the path you are taking, be relentless in your pursuit. Do not let rejection get you down—in the quest for the perfect job it's just par for the course. Other people will undoubtedly have had the same idea about getting their feet through a particular door, so prepare yourself for your toes to be stepped on during the process. Before I finally got my first dream job developing scripts for a film company, I spent years sending out a million resumes without receiving a single rejection letter. Were my phenomenal talents and supreme suitability for the positions going unrecognized? More likely, the companies concerned were so inundated they couldn't be bothered to write back. Don't take it personally. Persist, and eventually someone will give you an interview, and in the end, an offer.

Also remember to enjoy the ride. Life is about the journey; treating it as a competition will only end in tears. Think of success not in terms of what other people think about you, but how you perceive yourself. If you've tried your hardest and Lady Luck doesn't break your way, forgive yourself. At least you were brave enough to give it a try. Relish the freedom of only having yourself to consider, and appreciate how much more flexible you can be when all those new opportunities arise. You are not held hostage by what someone else requires of you—so go ahead, strive for your dream. Since you are single, doors are open to you that may be firmly closed later, such as working abroad for a period. One 29-year-old SG friend of mine recently went to work for a Prada-wearing devil of a fashionista in New York, something she would never have contemplated doing had she still been with her conventional ex-boyfriend. Not only would he have objected to the serial cocktail party demands on her time—he sent her to a cooking course because he thought her place was making, not eating, canapés—he suffered panic attacks when outside a two-mile radius of his soccer club.

Applying for a job can be a job in itself. You can buy books on recruitment, but be warned—my **GBF** was hired fresh out of college to write such tomes without having ever held, or indeed applied for, a full-time job.

The application process is basically common sense. A short and succinct covering letter helps, as does a relevant resume. A little embellishment goes a long way, as long as it's not too far-fetched. No one is actually going to check if you were president instead of secretary of your school's Literary Society; however, they might just look into your job as assistant to "Posh" Spice. For backup, offering "gifts" to your personal references is perfectly acceptable. One male friend offered his reference sexual favors; a meeting for drinks is usually sufficient.

On your employment search, there's no substitute for networking. Anyone can network, but being single, you have a massive advantage—you don't have to deal with mate maintenance and can devote appropriate attention to expanding your address book. I attend, on average, four evening events a week that will help my career. This may seem a lot, but then again I work in "fluffy" industries (by fluffy I refer to the walking cliché that is the "meeja"—that is, media—world and its members) where many involved don't do daylight hours. Actors and musicians are nocturnal creatures; they prefer to perform at night, since they then have half a chance of a captive audience and of manipulating the light to maintain their forever-youthful reputations.

If you know you have the skills and all you need is "the break," networking will in time come through for you. One A-list SG theater director I know who cultivated contacts left, right, and center stage eventually got her chance—a connection revealed she was resigning from a position that would be perfect for the SG director. They stood at a mailbox and sent their respective resignation and application letters together. The boss could not believe his luck when both letters appeared at the same time, saving him the hassle of recruiting anyone. The rest is award-laden history.

• THE INTERVIEW •

A wise acquaintance once said that interviews are about arriving at a mutually compatible set of lies—which is also a fitting description for a first date if ever I heard one. Since you will have invariably been sharpening your own such skills on the singles scene, you are also at a huge advantage here.

First, as on a date, dress in an outfit you know you can kick ass in, but make sure it's appropriate: Don't wear a short skirt and stilettos if they will distract you from impressing the interviewer (and interviewers from paying enough attention to your sharp comments rather than your shapely calves). One SG I know has the same uniform for a date as for an interview: trousers, high-heeled boots, and adjustable cleavage—the number of buttons done up or down depending on which tactics she has decided on for either encounter. Think about what employers are looking for and dress to fit their ideal. Your pin-stripe-tastic outfit for a job in a bank is not going to be the same as for one at a fashion magazine, where you will sweat or shiver in next season's must-have item (fashionistas work six months ahead, so their clothes cause inappropriate body temperatures). When you arrive, make sure your handshake is firm, neither limp nor ball-breaking, which are off-putting in any social setting. Also, maintain good eye contact—who wants someone in their office whose eyes are fixed on their feet, even if they are wearing very good shoes?

Then there are the searching questions about your views and actions, past and present. Respond as eloquently as you can, portraying yourself in the best possible light. A friend of mine who works in human resources typically asks the following: "What is the most difficult decision you have ever had to make?" One female candidate replied, "Deciding to go ahead with an abortion." Not the best subject matter for an interview (or indeed, first date). It was the only time my HR friend has ever been stunned into silence by an interviewee, who of course didn't get the job. So much of life, especially your working one, demands the ability to self-censor when required. You need to answer in a manner that will show off your suitability for the job, so always try to tie in replies to work-related matters.

Read the trade publications for the industry you are hoping to join and drop in some jargon. One SG friend went through twelve rounds of interviews with an American bank armed merely with a few relevant terms and the gift of the gab. I still doubt that she knows her bulls from her bears, but she remains in the position because she can sell a pension plan to anyone. Some firms care less about knowledge; the interview process is more about testing your survival skills. They will thus pride themselves on the number of pointless interviews they will put you through and the level of offensive questions they will ask. During one session at such a firm, a confidante of mine was asked to estimate how many gravediggers were currently working in the United Kingdom. She later found out her unfazed guess was the reason she was offered the job.

If you make minor errors, don't let them knock you off your stride—as on dates, mistakes can be endearing. One SG pal was in a job interview and nervously kept banging her foot against the table leg. She thought it was going well, as one of the guys interviewing her kept smiling; it was only at the end of the interview that she realized it was actually his leg, not the table's, that she had been knocking against. She was awarded the position, as was my SG fashion PR friend who said "blow job" instead of "blow dry" to a particularly attractive male interviewer.

Your interviewer wants to see some personality, so don't be afraid of letting yours shine through. Imagine you are the twentieth in a long line of interviewees and are asked by the rather bored head of HR, "What is your greatest achievement?" Rather than saying "Running the marathon," think of something a little more entertaining, like talking your way into the VIP section at an MTV Awards show and having Orlando Bloom admire your Kitson heels. Bring it back to work by saying how this displays your tenacity, as well as your spark. These people are going to have to spend at least nine hours a day with you, so they would undoubtedly prefer an interesting, lively addition to the team to someone dull and somewhat sanctimonious.

After you land The Job, you now have to manage your working life. Work/life balance can be tricky to achieve, but thankfully there are short cuts.

• BOSS MANAGEMENT •

Bosses are no different than parents, friends—indeed everyone and thing in your world—and need to be managed. Some call this manipulation, but there's nothing cruel about making sure that your world is running in an orderly manner. When the people in your life are playing to your tune, you are being effective, which is what a boss wants.

There tend to be two types of bosses—easy (usually male) and tricky (usually female). Male bosses are a bizarre mix of fathers and boyfriends, normally displaying typical traits of each. They can be wound round your little finger, but at the same time are prone to occasional bouts of unreasonable behavior. However, they are far less likely than the female of the species to hold a long-term grudge.

Male bosses are often concerned primarily with "style," that is, how things are perceived. Minutiae are normally not their game—they want the big picture first and, as long as the small stuff gets done are less likely to sweat about how you go about it. Most can be easily managed with friendly banter, brutal efficiency, and occasional flattery/flirting. (Note: flirting does not mean sleeping with, which is almost always a very bad idea. If you are having an affair with your boss, please refer to Chapter Eight.)

If you need a decision from, or something done by, a male boss, making him feel it's his idea is the quickest way forward. Be lavish in praise to your bosses, always emphasizing their importance to your good work, how you benefit from their mentoring (even if this is not wholly true). They will then magnanimously give you some credit where it is due. Become the mistress of the art of suggestion, such as planting the idea that you need funding for a new project/overtime/promotion. They will then either think the brainwave is all theirs and suggest it themselves, or be more amenable when you approach them about it. Accomplish this by e-mailing them a few very early morning or late evening messages, thus demonstrating your commitment, discussing with them how you feel you can improve, and subtly pointing out how well you compare to those just above you in the work pecking order. They should be putty in your hands. Some men are "old school" in outlook and have preconceived notions about women and their roles in the workplace. When a male boss's behavior becomes particularly objectionable, it can be a struggle to suppress the urge to drill a stiletto heel into his head. SGs can confuse these types of bosses, who sometimes think you're merely killing time while husband-hunting. But before you lift that stilettoed foot—*stop*. You can often turn these attitudes around to your advantage. You do not have to break down barriers; you are brighter than that. You will figure out how to walk around them.

For instance, men, specifically older ones, claim they are poor typists when they are actually perfectly proficient. I was once a useless secretary (high-level, just incompetent), and my boss would dictate his e-mails to me, as he claimed he was a slow, one-fingered typist. He was actually quite speedy, being caught out using as many as eight fingers at once on occasion.

I was initially irritated, but then realized I could profit from this. I was copied in on all high-level, confidential e-mails and learned a huge amount that came into seriously good use during subsequent job hunting, when it was clear that my knowledge could be a real asset to any potential employer. Of course, while I was still at the company, the information I was privy to meant that I was a proper power player. I may have had to make cups of tea for my boss, but I never had to make my own. The rest of the office pandered to my every hot drink need, and I often found copious quantities of chocolates on my desk. I knew of every major decision before everyone else; making me an ally became very useful to my co-workers. Whatever your boss's flaws, find a way to use them to your advantage.

If the male boss is about style, the female boss is about substance. They care about the minutiae *and* the big picture. That does not mean that they cannot be managed, just that it is harder, and unless you do it well, they will probably spot what you are up to a mile off. To get where they are, they will have played all the same games. Usually the female boss will be a cross between a particularly ugly sister and, if you are really unlucky, a step-monster with a grudge. Female bosses pay acute attention to detail, which means: Cover your back. If this is a challenging work environment where they need to be ruthless to survive, make sure you don't become the sacrificial cow.

It's essential that you keep them on your side. Thus, be meticulous in your dealings, so that mistakes that are not yours can never be attributed to you. Also, be conscientious in keeping female bosses in the loop—they like to know what is going on because they are thinking about everything that is going on—and deferential. Do not raise their hackles and antagonize their natural female competitive instinct by dressing in your most drop-dead gorgeous attire—keep it professional, otherwise it could be the kiss of career death. Never be seen with a better handbag, nor discuss your more functional love life, and under no circumstances ever flirt with their other halves. Although they might be the harder taskmistresses, they may well support you to the hilt when you really need it (especially if it will enhance their reputation). And you could get the female boss who is one of the occasional exceptions to the rule—one of mine still takes me out to dinner years after having worked for her.

• **COLLEAGUE MANAGEMENT** •

Common sense dictates that it is essential to keep anyone who works with you on your side. Not only does this make for a more pleasant working environment, but in the case of those who work under you, it also means they are more likely to accept the tasks you delegate to them (and cover your incompetence while buying you carbs if you are battling the hangover from hell). This allows you to e-mail and phone your friends—umm, I mean leave the office on time—and attain that elusive work/life balance.

Appearances are everything. Managing your working world means being perceived to be working at an effective but maximum capacity. Being overworked does no one nor any business any good, especially if you are in a job you do not like. You are single and do not want to be too exhausted to revel in your status after hours.

There are a number of tactics you can employ to make sure everyone knows you have reached maximum capacity without resorting to whining, which will just antagonize everyone around you. If you have a cell phone on which you can send and receive e-mail, make sure you fix the settings so that it will be clear to the recipient when you have sent a message from the device. For instance, every e-mail from an iPhone ends with the words "Sent from my iPhone." You should then send such missives at slightly obscure hours, as it will make you look extremely busy but nonetheless on top of things. If you get in to work early or stay late, make sure you e-mail key people as soon as you arrive or just before you depart, so they realize the hours you are putting in. And if you are getting overloaded in the office, send "holding" e-mails saying that you cannot resolve the query now, but it is on your mind. Wherever you go during working hours, make sure you are holding a piece of official-looking paper and wearing a purposeful expression. It will dawn on colleagues—eventually—that you're swamped, but that you're doing your best. They are then far more likely to come to your rescue than if you had thrown a hissy fit.

Appreciate your co-workers, no matter what their level is. The mailroom people, the IT guys, and the unpaid interns make the working world go round. Ensure they are invited to team lunches and for drinks, and remember their birthdays. Whether it's the coffee boy or personal assistant, look after them—not only yours, but other peoples' too. One associate of mine was brokering a deal with a particularly irritating attorney in New York. She befriended his executive assistant after discovering they both had a Daniel-Craig-dressed-in-trunks fetish. After clogging up their companies' e-mail systems sharing photos of the new James Bond, she found her calls were always returned and the deal was quickly done. One of my SG friend's PA is essential to my well-being, even getting me tables in fully-booked restaurants when only corporate pulling power will sway the maître d'. My SG friend rarely gets a Christmas card from me, but I always send her PA one.

The smallest kindness often fosters the biggest amount of good will, and food is the cheapest and easiest smile-maker. If you occasionally bring back candy from the deli, or cookies from Mrs. Fields for everyone to share, people will put themselves out that much more for you. When I organize a theater workshop, where everyone is giving his or her time for free, I always make sure there's plenty of delicious food. An actor's performance will inevitably scale shiny-statuette-worthy heights thanks to Gummi Bears and Hershey's Kisses.

Everyone exploits their own repertoire of skills. You are single, and some friendly flirtation is not going to hurt anyone as long as you don't cross professional lines. People do business with people who attract them in some way—financially and, indeed, personally. A stunning SG friend of mind who sacrificed supermodeling for stock brokering is regularly the only woman in meetings. She wears the smartest suits, the sharpest stilettos, and normally gets her way by flattering the men around her. Sometimes, of course, flirting will not get the required response. These men play the macho card and try to impose their way, at which point she is prepared to dig those heels in. She always arrives armed with a game plan, only concedes as much as she planned to before the meeting began, and finds the room typically acquiesces to her demands. If it does not, it needs to know my friend will walk away rather than be walked over. If she has to resort to this tactic, she almost always gets a phone call within hours agreeing to her proposal.

Work is not a place to display chinks in your armor, but some colleagues will try to find them, no matter how many chocolate chip cookies you hand out. However wound up you get, never let them see you cry, even if you are shouted at (that is what bathroom breaks are for). Since you're single, some colleagues will decide this is the topic they can tease you about. Your refusal to settle in the wrong relationship shows strength of character, but many people who have not exercised such good sense are threatened by this and will try to use it against you. Valentine's Day is a particularly obnoxious holiday, when work colleagues (especially those who have just added a piece of jewelry to the third finger of their left hands) become unbearable. With the good manners that they have failed to extend to you by flagrantly flaunting their attached status, cordially congratulate them, while quietly remembering that any occasion demanding delight as a prerequisite rarely is one—even if it involves presents or sex. The SG holds the upper hand on Valentine's Day; no expectation means no disappointment. Be glad you're not the girl whose long-term boyfriend delivers nothing more than some dead flowers from the local supermarket. If you want to fight back by showing off something tangible from someone who loves you, employ the reciprocal arrangement, whereby you and a friend send each other a delivery of flowers/chocolates/gift of your choosing to the office, and when it arrives you can be as mysterious as you like. Attached people will get jealous—remember, being single means that everything is possible. You may still end up with Leo DiCaprio; they cannot, as they have settled for Wayne from IT.

You may also be sharing the office with the "proud parents," those who never tire of talking about their little ones. They remind you regularly their children are the reasons they're late for work, looking a mess, taking extra time off, and so on. Coo over their pictures when you need something from them; otherwise, remain silent and get your vacation requests in early. If these parents are really getting to you, go out during lunch, buy a new pair of shoes, and proceed to show them off to everyone round the office when you get back, leaving them to look forlornly at their lunchtime purchase—diapers from Duane Reade.

• WORK EVENTS •

Although there is a chapter specifically on Event Management, work events are so entwined with work politics that a discussion of them has to go here. As mentioned above, the dream job, deal, or project is liable in some way to result from networking. If you are seen at the right events, talk to the right people, and make the right contacts, it will eventually pay off—and you could even find yourself having fun along the way. Contacts can come from the most obscure places. While working on a theater project, I found the perfect director when I stepped on his toe at midnight at a party. The project in question had come about after I met the writer's agent in a gay night-club in Marrakech on New Year's Eve while dancing to Madonna's "Hung Up". If I had spent both nights going **Big Duvet**, in bed under the covers, as I'd been tempted to do, my career—and indeed my life—would have turned out very differently.

Whatever your industry, there will be social events. It is essential for your own benefit to go for at least a few official after work drinks, but you certainly do not need to attend all of them; a little forethought and you can always excuse your absence. Betrothed and baby-in-tow colleagues have their own standard covers for excusing themselves from work events, but SGs also have certain tricks at their disposal. If the gathering is not only going to be dire, but will also fail to help you climb the career ladder in any way, say that you cannot make it because you are "at the theater/opera." Never the movies or on a date, both of which in many people's minds are cancelable activities. This way you're far less likely to be challenged when you change for the outing in the bathroom at work and totter back through the office catwalk in your hottest ensemble.

For the more useful social events on the work calendar, your presence does not have to be negotiated with a disagreeable other half or demanding child. Your evenings are your own, and if you want to attend, you can. Furthermore, on the occasions you do choose to grace a work event with your presence, everyone will be suitably grateful, as you can be relied on to "give good value." Let me explain.

SGs can always make the time to shine. Unlike more relationship responsibility overloaded colleagues, you can do some extra homework before you arrive at the affair. Research who is going, why, and what they want from the event. Work out what you yourself need to gain from the gathering and compile a **Conversation List (CL)**. This should include a number of questions for you to ask and a list of replies to inquiries that might be made of you. The CL does not have to be something you write down—it can simply be a thought process—but it is an invaluable tool in many areas of life; a steering mechanism to keep discussions on a track you're comfortable with. Your prior preparation means that there are never any embarrassing pauses in conversation—unless it serves your purposes—and it's easier to procure any pertinent information you may need from the rendezvous. Just a small dose of cool, calculated conversation management is all that's required to achieve your desired outcome from the gathering.

It is rare for SGs to find that our sex and sexuality—our (relatively) youthful good looks and single status—do not become a factor at evening events; indeed they can make these occasions a veritable minefield. We deal with crossing the "work-colleague line" in later chapters, but with some forward planning, including a CL, a safe path can usually be negotiated through work events.

Example: my supermodel stockbroker friend is regularly invited by a lawyer associate to accompany him to the opera, where his firm has sponsored seats. She suspects he is infatuated, but thanks to her groundwork—the CL, the high-necked and ankle-skimming outfits, and the escape strategy (pre-ordered car service)—the possibility of him making inappropriate advances is greatly reduced. At meals with her office colleagues, she always leaves immediately after the dinner, before all the men on her team decide to go to a strip club. This sort of situation is something we all have to deal with to some degree, whether it means fending off someone on an overnight business trip or leaving the boys you work with at the bar to get seriously trashed once you've had your swift after-work sharpener with them. You are free—to stay out with them or go home and curl up with a tub of Ben & Jerry's and *Point Break* if you so desire. All useful networking will have taken place before you leave anyway—men tend to get memory loss by the third pint.

If you are a single female, the business lunch or dinner provides another test—especially if you are the only woman there. Your companions may be less sure about how to pitch their behavior if confronted with a together, gorgeous SG in such an intimate social setting, so you need to take control and make sure they cross no inappropriate boundaries. It is all too easy to make the wrong impression. At the end of one meal, a particularly bubbly SG friend's boss had mistaken her friendliness for a come-on and asked her up to his hotel room to "drink the mini-bar dry." Unlike during an interview, which has all the hallmarks of a date, if you are at a work meal, keep in mind how you behave. You're not with a potential lover, so act accordingly. Coyly deliberating with your companion about what you want to eat will make you look indecisive; if you tend to get in a flux every time you see a menu, try looking up the restaurant's offerings on the Internet first so you can choose beforehand. It is vital for appearances' sake to order your easy-to-eat courses (you don't want to be slathering spaghetti over your chin) within seconds, close your menu, and quickly steer discussions into work areas. Note here that if you eat red meat, a rare steak will do wonders for your killer instinct reputation—one SG I know was recruited because she ordered hers bloody. Do not have dessert unless the rest of the table decides to first, as you will otherwise risk being seen as a time waster. Try to stay sober, or at least interchange wine with water. Work events are just that—work—and they need to be orchestrated. Getting drunk and wrapping a loose tongue around a date is one thing; having a loose tongue at a work event is something else entirely.

If partners are invited to the event, be careful when dealing with your colleagues' and with choosing your "plus one." Do not invite either a professional escort or a **Social Hand Grenade** to your party. The former will always be found out; the latter will inevitably create difficulties if you abandon them, even for an instant. One SG friend left her mischievous platonic male "plus one" while she went to powder her nose; when she returned everyone at the table was looking at her oddly. She later discovered he had told them that she had always fancied him and that, apart from a one-night stand when they had done it doggy style, she really wasn't his type. The girl left the company soon after.

It is probably best, after initial pleasantries have been exchanged, to politely ignore your female work colleagues' partners; you don't want any light banter to be misconstrued by the women you work with as flirting. When it comes to your male colleagues' other halves, you must ensure that these women know that you are not a threat, and you are not going to have an affair with their husband/boyfriend in the workplace. You are a glamorous SG, and that will naturally disturb them—you will be spending more hours with their partners than they do. They will think you fancy their husbands even when for you it would be a physical impossibility; remember, they find them attractive in some way, even if you never could, so tread carefully around them. They perceive you as a predator, and thus you have no margin of error in your dealings with other halves. Never ask what she does or when the baby is due, unless you are absolutely sure that she does have a job or that she is pregnant. One of my friends, a fresh-faced recruit recently out of college, was at a work drinks party where the wine was flowing and some exceedingly good honey and mustard sausage canapés were making the rounds. She asked the boss's wife, "When is it due?" The older woman was momentarily confused and then replied, "Oh, I am not pregnant! I'm just fat". Fresh-faced recruit eventually left the company—for some strange reason she never received a promotion. If the person inquiring had been carrying post-baby weight or partner-padding too (matching a boyfriend's eating habits plays havoc on the waistline), the faux pas would have been laughed off and quickly forgotten.

Occasionally it will be impossible to convince these women you are not after their man. There is an extreme, but nevertheless true, example of a journalist confidante of mine who got fired because the wife of her particularly ugly boss decided she was having an affair with him. This was absolutely ridiculous—he looked like an old, fat frog, and my beautiful journalist friend was madly in lust with a smooth-bodied Adonis. The boss's wife began calling journo-girl up at all hours, even while she was in bed with the Greek god, and then threatened to hit her when she ran into her at a work function.

Once you've survived your work event, always e-mail, or better yet write a real-life thank you note, as soon as possible to whomever organized the occasion. Also, drop a line to people whose business cards you have collected. Occasionally it pays to organize get-togethers yourself, although it is an error to be the one who always does it. You don't want to burden yourself with unnecessary responsibility. People should be pleasantly surprised if you arrange something, aware that your single status means you will always have something—or someone—better to do.

Despite all these guidelines, it is, of course, possible to mess up, and there is one place that is more of a minefield than most . . .

• THE OFFICE CHRISTMAS PARTY •

If you can get through the Christmas period without getting drunk at least once, you have nerves of steel. For all parties, but especially the office one, I suggest sticking to champagne (if by some miracle the boss splashes out for some); hopefully the budget will be Scrooge-like enough to swiftly run out and you will not have to drink any more. Plus there will come a point when everyone else is so drunk they will not notice that you have moved on to the sparkling water with ice and lemon.

In the UK (and I suspect in America as well), the most badly behaved person is usually the boss. Stories of their horrific festive behavior are innumerable. A secretary I know has to order her boss a "vomit cab"—some firms, for a vast puke premium, supply them during the merry season for passengers they would normally refuse owing to their indecent level of inebriation.

How you use your single freedom during this period is up to you—you have the option of taking the seasonal spirit much further than those who are attached, and are allowed to indulge in physical encounters with the opposite sex. However, it helps if he is single too and if you would be happy to lunge at him in any other month. If he would make your blood run cold in January, a mistletoe moment in December is not going to warm the heart for any longer than it takes for the hangover to kick in.

Accidents will happen this time of year. Keep your cell handy to take pictures of any scandalous behavior from your co-workers (in case you need to bribe someone not to shout about your own), plan your exit strategy, and get out as soon as possible. It's all over for another year, and you can spend the coming months getting your body beautiful back in shape.

WORK MANAGEMENT

Survival Tips

- Get a job of some description. Every SG needs a raison d'être to get out of bed...and disposable income for shoes.
- Pre-bound into a better job. It's always easier to find work if you're already employed. SGs don't rebound, we're better than that.
- Network: good things come to those out and about.
- Bribery in the form of buying communal candy for co-workers will make your working world that much sweeter.

CHAPTER 2

Mind over Matter Management

*I*F WE LOOK fabulous, we feel fabulous. If we feel fabulous, we *are* fabulous. As an SG, you can concentrate wholeheartedly on sorting *you* out from top to toe, inside and out. We can devote a plentiful proportion of our time to the body beautiful—to our physical and mental health, our grooming—our very being. We have enough energy to ensure we are in peak condition and are time-rich enough to address the essential (making that appointment we've been postponing to deal with a nagging ailment) to the frivolous—but nevertheless important—anti-aging treatment that a manic mom or stressed spouse might not have time to perform.

For the time being we are not sharing our bathrooms with large, smelly Neanderthals whom we have to hide hair removing cream from. We have the disposable cash to buy products with pretty packaging and organic health food that makes us feel virtuous despite a vodka overindulgence the night before. We can treat ourselves to learning a new trivial (or positively practical) pursuit—flying or salsa lessons, or simply to a massage at a beauty spa. Lavish attention on yourself—this is your moment to indulge. You will never again be as young as you are or look as good as you do right now, so enjoy it. Yes, it is important to be realistic—we are never going to look like one of the airbrushed creatures in magazines (OK, I've had it done in one photo—see book cover)—but in truth, as I can absolutely attest, these pictures have been digitally altered to the extent that the models can barely recognize themselves in them. It is all about managing what you have got, to give you the confidence to live your life the way you want to. And, as Uma Thurman's Swedish goddess of a character in *The Producers* sings, when you've got it . . . flaunt it.

• **MORTAL MANAGEMENT** •

Your physical and mental health are the most vital things you will ever manage and are inextricably linked: a happy state of mind can promote good health. Not only are both these qualities essential to your maximum enjoyment of SG status, they will also ward off problems in time to come. As the SG now flourishes into her thirties and beyond, she may wish to reserve the right to have a child later in life. It's absolutely laudable to wait until the conditions are right in your world (the right mindset, and the right partner) for producing happy children; however, this makes it vital that you look after your body now. One girlfriend of mine gave herself the 35th birthday present of having some of her eggs frozen. Extremely sensible. Given her track record of boyfriends, inflicting an innocent child with any of the paternal candidates she has dallied with (so far) would be downright cruel.

If you are sick, being single is an additional strain; there is no one with whom you can automatically share your strife. Don't forget you have friends and family who will be there to help—so if you feel the need, ask for it. You would do the same for them. However, if you're trying to establish a prognosis, you may not want to worry anyone, and at this point, there are some SG tactics to employ.

The most crucial CLs the SG will ever create are for doctors. Remember that doctors do not know everything; this became apparent when I met people trying to become them at college. Seeing my contemporaries qualify made me realize doctors are human—and fallible—and it began to dawn on me it may be wise to manage the medical "profession." My GP's office is right across the street from my old school. Every time I see him, my legs turn to jelly and I feel like a talentless teenager again. (That school seems to have left similar scars on all its ex-pupils, or my friends at least—one craves cider whenever she walks past it, while another will take a detour rather than risk a run-in with the fearsome French teacher.) From my bitter experience of always being in a nervous state when I see the doctor, thus never being able to ask the right questions, I now write down and take in a list of queries and then diligently take notes from his answers. To help me compose an effective CL, I glean some of my information from the Web (although do not always believe what you read), and other material from my friends. If you think you will not be able to take in anything a doctor says—like when I discovered a lump in my breast—bring a confidante to do the asking and listening. And please note, however tempting it may be, self-medicating is never clever—one SG I know actually answered a spam e-mail to buy Viagra online, having read that combined with a vibrator it would generate an orgasm unlike any other she had ever experienced. It was: the incident was more organ-numbing than earth-moving. Every cloud has a silver lining, though—the junior doctor dealing with her case did have a touch of "the Clooneys" about him, and when she got over her embarrassment she thoroughly enjoyed (all of) him.

Along with your CL, remember to consider your underwear; I once went for a scan and was wearing a Snoopy G-string. You will find medical experts immune to hairy legs and sprouting bikini lines, but a grinning Snoopy from your crotch area will surprise even the most straight-laced of professionals.

Probably the worst doctor experience you will come across at this stage of your life is the gynecologist. Not only can such encounters be painful, but as an SG, you may well have had sex with more than one partner since your last visit and would rather not regale a stranger with your sexual habits. If the person on the other side of the desk is acting like Mother Superior, remember it's not their business to give you a morality lesson. As long as you are happy and healthy (which is what you are there to confirm or attain), it doesn't matter what they think. Besides, however promiscuous you are, they will have seen patients who are *much* more so than you.

It is only natural that you may sometimes feel isolated when you want to discuss serious life issues. If there was a social stigma attached to having a therapist, it's long gone. There are many different types—from those with official medical qualifications to lifestyle coaches—and to some, they are a veritable accessory. One SG I know goes to a business therapist merely because of the contacts she picks up in the waiting room. She even dated a man she met by the water cooler, but had to ditch him because he yelled out "show me the money!" at every opportunity, including during sex.

If you can afford to do it, paying someone to listen to you has distinct advantages. You can focus more of your time with your friends on playing and less on bending their ears. Another SG, a stressed out model booker, credits her weekly therapy sessions for how she is generally in control of her world and the starving, bitchy people in it. If something upsets her, she decides to deal with it in her assigned therapy hour. Often when she gets to her appointment she cannot remember why she was so perturbed in the first place, and she and her therapist have a good gossip. Before she had a shrink, she loathed her tendency to get a bit weepy mid-week; now that she has it in check, she feels more in control and happier in general.

The first session with any therapist is always the worst, as you have to explain what has brought you to their door. Usually it's smoother sailing after you've outlined your issues, but if for some reason it's not, find another therapist. I was told I was anorexic and sent into therapy when I actually had a thyroid problem (doctors have been known to misdiagnose). I walked out on the first two therapists, as I felt they failed to listen. Therapist three thought to question the anorexia diagnosis itself—and only then was the real problem discovered and dealt with.

• ALTERNATIVE THERAPY •

Alternative practitioners—from masseuses and mediums to gurus—are other options the SG can consider in the battle for good health. Remember, you have only one body, so, as with doctors, scrutinize any alternative health practitioner's records carefully, giving most weight to any personal recommendations you have. It's your right (nay, your responsibility) to be fussy. Many of these therapists are rapidly becoming the norm—witness Gwyneth Paltrow's "cupping," a form of alternative pain therapy—but be wary of the "guru" gurus: those who preach the benefits of alternative religions such as scientology, auras, **Horrorscopes,** and so forth. These remain less socially acceptable for a reason, and you, the SG, are a prime target, since you are without partner and tweenagers to laugh you out of being drawn in by them. By the same token, be wary that, as an SG, you do not use an "expert", whether self- or degree-acclaimed, to fill a perceived gap in your world and then let them dictate how you should live your life. It took months for me and my friends to convince an SG who had been ordered by a "nutritionist" to only eat raw food that there is nothing wrong with the odd steak dinner or glass of red wine. It was only when our friend literally turned orange (because of the number of carrots she was consuming) that she resumed normal vodka, lime, and soda duty. Remember, you are looking for balance, not additional stress because you're unable to follow a bizarre regimen, so take from them what works for you. Pause and listen to what your body is telling you, then research how best you can help it.

• SURFACE MANAGEMENT •

You're beautiful inside; now for the outside. As an SG, you have those spare minutes in the day, and the disposable cash, to be the envy of your married/attached friends who have babies and males eating into their hair-drying and bra-buying time. You can make getting your skin smooth, assembling a becoming wardrobe, and applying your make up flawlessly a priority.

In creating your body beautiful, a GBF is essential. It may be a stereotype, but it is one friends-of-Dorothy consistently live up to—every Grace can use a Will, and all Wills love having a Grace to boss around. The GBF will be honest about what you are wearing/ how fat you are/your cellulite, things a woman rarely says, either because she doesn't want to offend or doesn't want a harsh retort.

In my experience, the GBFs have the number (on speed dial) of the best waxer in town—men have thicker hair and are male, so they have a lower pain threshold. Of course, being single, you can go for the painless "Italian option"—fabulous on the outside, a gorilla underneath (as the author Kathy Lette says, it's the only time it is ever socially acceptable to proclaim "bring back Bush"). A Brazilian bikini wax hurts however many Advils you pop, but you don't have to do it unless it makes you feel better about yourself.

This type of quick fix can extend to other areas, for instance only self-tanning your face and bits on display.

Good bedside manners should extend from physicians to beauticians. When you enter a beauty salon, do not let a tyrannical consultant alarm you by insisting you need more services than you've booked, or that you should purchase a truckload of products from them that you will never use. There is also no need for embarrassment on your part, even if you are ordered onto your hands and knees on their treatment table half naked with your bottom in the air so they can reach some tricky tufts of hair. They have seen worse ingrown hairs, thicker bikini lines, and bigger, more bunioned feet. Just make sure your nooks and crannies are clean when you submit yourself to their hands. You are paying and possibly (absolutely in the case of a good waxer) tipping them, so if they make you feel uncomfortable, find new ones.

Be slightly wary if your beautician comes from another land, or you are having a treatment abroad—matters can get lost in translation. There is no international language of waxing, so be as specific as possible. (Also ensure that your waxer is properly trained by inquiring as to their qualifications and experience—third-degree burns are not worth a discount, nor the mirth of your latest lover.) To a European therapist, a Brazilian wax means leaving a landing strip remaining, but to a waxer from Hollywood, it means everything off. I know this first hand, as I was left bald in a place I felt should have a little hair when a La-La Land therapist got her hands on me at my local London salon.

Along with the treatments themselves, socially acceptable salon behavior differs on every continent. While on a business trip to LA, I popped to the hotel spa and was confronted with a disclaimer form asking if I used recreational drugs *or* alcohol—in the same sentence. In my mind, a glass of red wine is completely different from **hoovering** a vast quantity of cocaine, but obviously not to Angelenos. Turn up to a massage in Thailand stark naked as you would in Sweden and you will find no oil in sight, just a very small and resolute looking woman waving a pair of pyjamas for you to dress in. She will then proceed to bend you into positions you never thought possible outside the Kama Sutra. As in everything, do as much research as you can before you enter the doors of any salon or spa.

Most of your beauty routine will of course take place in your own bathroom. This is your "safety zone," where you can make honest assessments about your look. If your makeup is the same as it was five years ago, find a friend who does hers fabulously to instruct you how to change it. One SG I know had been using the same make-up suggestions she got from a teen magazine she read when she was 14 (SG was now 33). An imperious but well-groomed 23-year-old finally had to step in and overhaul SG's face-paint routine. Also, don't feel like you need to break the bank to makeover to your heart's content. A store brand shampoo can leave your hair as silky smooth as a Saks one. If a salon is charging fifty dollars to cut cuticles, do that bit at home, and go for the ten dollar professional revarnish. Opt for a store-bought, do- it-yourself facial from Duane Reade, and with the money saved splurge on a chair massage, something that you could definitely not manage to perform yourself.

Focus on what makes you feel good in your own body. I like my hands, so it's rare that my nails look anything less than painted perfection. But I hate my pale bluish skin, so I am never seen baring flesh without a spray tan (my impression of a recently plucked chicken does not have to be inflicted on the world). Feeling good is like a performance-enhancing drug. When I sat for my final exams in college, we all turned up looking a mess, apart from one girl who arrived in bohemian glory and glittery eye make-up. We all thought she was mad—those ten minutes she had spent grooming we had spent cramming. She said that she always got better results if she felt good about herself. Glitter Girl was one of the few women to get top honors in my subject that year; none of my cramming circle did. Not a day goes by when I don't remember her lesson. If a confidence boost is required, put on that extra layer of lip gloss and a pair of higher heels.

• PROCEDURES •

With the advent of injections and lasers, the goalposts on what defines cosmetic surgery are forever moving. As it gets more advanced and more affordable (both Botox and blemish-removal can cost less than an advanced facial), it's also becoming more socially acceptable. Some who claim they would never have a facelift get Botox injections; others have unsightly veins and blemishes lasered while scoffing at anyone who uses injected filler. Then there is laser eye surgery, which in the long run is cheaper than contacts and new frames. Are these important health-improving operations or mere vanity projects?

Don't worry about what other people think. Most of the time they won't notice the defects that you do (or the tricks that you perform to conceal or correct them.). However, if you decide fixing a flaw will make you feel better about yourself and let you hold your head that much higher, and you can budget for it, do it. Make sure you find a reputable physician. One 50-something SG (well, she could be anywhere between 40 and 70) regularly disappears to New York to get her skin freshened and veins zapped for less than five hundred dollars. It would cost double that in the UK, and with less than state of the art techniques being used. As with any service, make sure you do your research, and only part with your cash for the best.

Timing is also key. One school friend of mine with a distinguished nose came back with a small perky one after the summer holidays. Even at 17, she had great timing. It's very hard to get work done in your home town without it being noticed afterward. Even if you only nip to the corner store, news of your every tuck will spread like wildfire, though as an SG you don't have to worry about your other half getting drink and spilling the beans.

Surgery should always be a last resort as there are serious risks, from a botched op that gives you a trout pout, to landing in intensive care. So try creams and, in the case of various body parts, exercise first. Personal trainers are always a cheaper fat-burning option than liposuction under a general anaesthetic, and a lesser danger to your person.

• EXERCISE •

Fitness is no longer about wearing green gym suits and being picked on during Phys Ed by bullying girls. I was always the last to be selected for teams at school owing to my uselessness at everything athletic. This put me off such activity for years. Eventually I mustered up the courage to enter a gym in my early 20s, discovering that by no means was I the most pathetic member. Now I bet I can do more abdominal crunches than anyone from my graduating class.

Exercise means you get to do what suits you, and in quite fetching sports gear. But there is never any point in setting the exercise bar so high that you won't be inspired to clamber over it. You need to be realistic about what you can fit in and what activity is right for you. It may be power walking around the park with a dog or your **BF**. It may be a yoga class, where you can gossip with fellow yogi in between downward dogs. It may be biking to work. However, for many a busy SG with an aversion to battling the weather when somewhere warm will perfectly suffice, it will be pounding the treadmill of the gym, plugged into your iPod and ignoring the world for forty minutes. (As a superior SG, though, you know that to shock your body slim you need to mix up the cardio with some weight work and turn some of your mass into muscle to quicken your metabolism).

When joining a gym, do not be swayed in your selection by fluffy towels or handsome gym instructors (do you want them to see you at your sweaty worst anyway?). Your gym choice is all about location. I once belonged to a gym a 15-minute walk away. When it was cold and damp out, I struggled to get there. I now go to one 30 seconds away from my apartment and make it there almost every day, even if it's just for twenty minutes. The marginally more remote exercise emporium may have been more luxurious, but it was no competition for my bed. Note that if you join such an establishment in January as a result of a New Year's resolution, please do not be put off if you have to do battle with crowds of people to use the equipment. Come February, you'll have the place to yourself.

If you choose a gym attended by no one you know, you can take on an alternative persona. However, if the club is by the office, due care and attention will be called for. I once worked for a record company, and it was compulsory among staff to like indie (cutting edge) music, but I prefer my tunes somewhat more fromage-tastic, especially when working out—New Kids being so much easier to feel the burn to than Nickelback. We all went to the gym next door, so I used to plug into the club's shared sound system, listen to cheesy songs on a very cheesy radio station, and then switch the little box on my treadmill to an indie station before I got off. The one time I forgot, the head of A&R (the department that goes out and finds the talent) never forgave me, even going as far as sending a disparaging e-mail about my music choice to my head of department. One petty turn deserves another, so every time I did weights near him, when I was done, I would change the settings so they were far heavier than I would ever bother to lift. When he sat down to do them he was suitably freaked out at how superior my skills were to his own. He was also the type that had a favorite cross-trainer, which I would try to make sure I beat him to and then spend an inordinate time on so he was forced to use another one. Alas, it seems that on entering the gym, all dignity is checked at the door, and you find yourself in a parallel universe where previously sane people become utter nutters. Indeed, it is somewhat awkward meeting fellow members outside the gym, as people tend to behave so differently—a whole Attenborough wildlife series could be devoted to the various types who inhabit this strange, often subterranean, environment.

Personal trainers are amazing—*if* you can afford them. Like therapists and friends, you need to be picky, so research by asking around at the gym which one will be best for you. If you don't like the one you choose, change. Girl personal trainers normally work girls harder, and of course you then remove the danger of dealing with any sexual advances . . . unless they (or you) are of the Martina Navratilova persuasion. Among my SG circle, a disproportionate number who have employed male trainers have ended up falling for their charms (or perhaps their muscle-y arms). Indeed, one SG friend, who had taken to incessantly texting her hunky instructor while she was away on a boat, caused the suitor who was subsidizing their holiday to get so jealous that he dropped her phone into the sea. There is something special about someone finding you attractive when you feel you are at your least, so if the wandering hands add a welcome frisson to your workout, go along with it. Just be wary of the dangers. When the love affair dies and/or they transfer to LA Fitness out of state, you may find eating chocolate and burrowing into your bed for a Big Duvet moment a more attractive alternative to the scene of the heartbreak. Nestlé might appreciate your state of distress, but your hips will not.

Gym locker rooms are bound to make you feel better about your body, as the lighting is so unforgiving it shows up everyone's cellulite. However, there is no need for you to be either a) one of those freaks who has a very complicated dressing routine with their towel wrapped firmly around them fearful of displaying anything (we have all seen it all before), or b) just the opposite, i.e. parading around absolutely stark naked. Like everything else in life, think balance!

• DIETS •

At this point, let us acknowledge a basic fact: diets, whether they be "cabbage patch" or "in the zone," are dull. And they make *you* duller. Of course, if you choose to eat everything that tempts you, you will be fat and unhealthy. Being too thin can be just as bad—and it shows up your wrinkles. We all know you are what you eat, that you should eat five portions of fruit and vegetables a day, that alcohol is full of calories, and cake, is too. We also know that, for most people, if you eat less and exercise more, you will eventually lose weight. It's not rocket science, although the diet industry tries to persuade us otherwise.

Instead of "dieting," look for lower calorie options when you go out to eat. Or meet people for drinks and not dinner, and then stop drinking alcohol after the first two glasses (people do not notice after a certain point in the evening whether you are on the lime and soda with or without the vodka). One SG I know has a maximum weight she is happy in herself with, and if she exceeds it, she quietly spends 20 minutes extra on the treadmill during her workouts and has hot, mashed up Weetabix (think Shredded Wheat) either for lunch or dinner. She is back to her comfortable weight within a week. The less difficult you make a diet, the more likely you are to lose those pounds.

When you're dieting, fellow females and gay men will often try to sabotage your regime to make them feel less guilty about theirs, while straight men will get bored and even annoyed if you refuse to eat. Since as an SG you can eat what you want, you are much less likely to be swayed by anyone else's need for munchies and can stock your fridge with what you like. If you are having a proper lunch and only want a chocolate bar for breakfast and cereal for dinner before or after you go out, you can. You do not have another half demanding you cook cajun chicken and crepes for two.

If you do diet, don't shout about it. Just do it.

• RETAIL THERAPY •

When an SG, you have the privilege of purchasing the items *you* feel are essential. Clothes and shoes are your uniform, and if you want, you can categorize them as the most pressing acquisitions to be made. Accessories—for example, a cutting-edge handbag swinging from your shoulder, make you interesting—both to other women and to men (gay ones will notice the style, straight ones your innate air of confidence). One older SG friend never shopped for herself unless her clothes had fallen apart because her husband made her feel too guilty. When he left her, she credits a new handbag with helping her get through some hazardous events solo. It looks better on her arm than he ever did.

Shoes are spectacular inventions. You can go crazy with them, whatever your figure and however much you currently weigh. They're also a fairly safe investment, unlike a too-small designer dress that will immediately date. Selecting a shoe can be like selecting a man, just without the emotional trauma, and, in the case of my divorced SG friend, they are cheaper. You can opt for the dull but dependable variety, or a sexy pair that you know will hurt you before too long but look oh-so-good. Plus there's the added bonus that you can walk all over them (in them, at least) and they're still around for more.

If in doubt about your sartorial style, consult any "Will" you can find. I will never forget arriving in skin-tight white jeans, a cleavage-revealing top, and mega platform heels at the office of my most high-powered GBF (a Palace of Westminster power player—a friend of my parents I have known since birth) so he could escort me to a party. He looked me up and down, and said, as loudly as possible, so that all the important people (well, politicians and their apparatchiks) in the vicinity could hear, "It is a bit Liz Hurley, isn't it?"

I learned my lesson. Never feel coerced into being a slave to fashion. Wear what suits you. If you have short legs, sandals with straps that go halfway up them will only accentuate them. If you are prone to being swayed into purchasing errors by pushy shop assistants, take your GBF for protection. He will tell you the truth far better than any mirror or commission brown-noser, as well as also encouraging you to take justified risks. While I was sitting down having a "tired-of-shopping in four-inch heels" time-out, my GBF spotted an evening dress I never thought I could fit into or get away with wearing and manhandled me into it. It is a show-stopper, although he does have to come round to arrange my breasts into it every time I want to wear it out.

• GOING ON VACATION •

Vital to an SG's vitality is occasionally giving yourself a break to keep mind, body, and soul in order. Yet another blessing for the SG is that you're not restricted by a partner's preferences. A vacation can be just that, not a "compromise" trip that will leave you shivering and shattered on a soccer tour in Iceland when you would have preferred to be on a beach. Your SG freedom may also allow you to go "out of season," when prices are cheaper and there are fewer families around. This in turn will make your vacation that much more peaceful, as you will not be doing battle with screaming youngsters who splash chlorine in your hair every time you enter the peed-in pool.

Another option is to go away with other singles. Choose your companions carefully. It is always a good idea to put forward your very specific idea of a perfect holiday while it is in the planning stage. If your friends like running around looking at monuments, while your favored activity is crawling toward a cocktail on the beach, perhaps you're not compatible break buddies. One SG friend of mine arrived in Ibiza, Spain, for some gentle sunning and instead was confronted with friends who had metamorphosed into coke-crazed clubbers. If in doubt, and the budget can stretch for it, at least opt for separate rooms.

Perhaps one of the last bastions of bravery for some is the single vacation alone. For this, the spa is perfect, because it will be full of other singles. I have several friends who go out every night at home but then reach the point where they cannot talk to anyone else. They regularly disappear for pampering at these places so they can become at peace with the world and clamber back on top of it again. Others sometimes declare they have gone away on vacation, but instead go into hibernation mode at home. They switch off their phones, stock up the fridge, and only venture as far as their duvets allow.

The main issue for people thinking about going away alone is dinner. At a spa there will always be an official "singles" table, but if joining the **Joiners** (Joiners are team players who relish outdoor group activities whatever the weather and are advocates of "enforced fun") fills you with dread, take a book. Though you may be feeling anti-social, remember that you may be surprised at whom you might meet. One girl I know met her husband at such a retreat, while I met someone who was to become one of my best financial backers in my work. We almost ended up lovers after meeting quite by chance over a bottle of wine with our spa cuisine one night (we were feeling rebellious—detoxing always makes me want to retox). Then we discovered he knew my father's BF and was also the father of one of my half-brother's school friends . . . Any thoughts of a romantic encounter were swiftly abandoned.

However much we may dream of being away from it all on indefinite vacation, we do have to go back to reality, and to our home. So let's turn our attention to managing the SG's domestic domain.

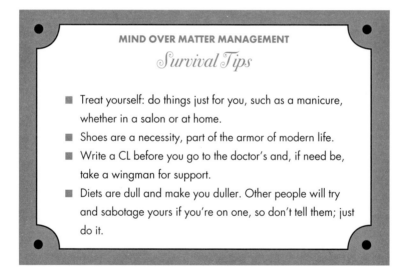

MIND OVER MATTER MANAGEMENT

Survival Tips

- Treat yourself: do things just for you, such as a manicure, whether in a salon or at home.
- Shoes are a necessity, part of the armor of modern life.
- Write a CL before you go to the doctor's and, if need be, take a wingman for support.
- Diets are dull and make you duller. Other people will try and sabotage yours if you're on one, so don't tell them; just do it.

CHAPTER 3

Home Management

HOME MAY BE where the heart is if you are a desperate housewife. It needn't be when you are a content bachelorette. Instead, where you reside can be whatever you decree it to be—a place only big enough to lay your head, or somewhere to hang out and throw legendary parties in.

Your place is not about physical space but mental space. I have multiple SG friends who happily live in shoeboxes so small they would have nowhere to store vast quantities of footwear even if they could afford to buy out Blahnik. Why? Because as much as they love their parents, they used to live with them. There is a reason girls leave home earlier than boys, even though it will stretch them financially just as much—guilt. (Yes, that emotion which womankind does *so* well.) Since boys fail to notice emotional blackmail as much, they end up receiving less of it. Parents simply give up giving them grief. Girls thus choose to flee the nest earlier. One **Girl Playmate** of mine has three lazy brothers, all over the age of 28 and all still living at home. She decamped at 21, but is still the person, after her parents, whom the police would call should the burglar alarm be activated. (Her brothers have been known to sleep through intruder alerts.)

Moving to my own miniature abode, away from living next door to two of my parents, gave me one of the best gifts I have ever had: an adult relationship with them. It's about as functional a relationship as one can get with blood, but it proved elusive when they could see and hear my every coming and going. Most of my claustrophobia at the set-up was undoubtedly in my own head, though the CCTV camera that was trained on my parents' front door (and by extension, mine) was wired up to their television set. I became convinced they sometimes watched their very own "Big Brother" channel, if the only alternative was a *Jerry Springer* rerun. One of my parents had developed a tendency to poke his head out of the kitchen window to say "hello" to my visitors and even once woke the neighbors up with his noisy teasing when he saw me tottering home from my then-boyfriend's early one morning. In his eyes he was, of course, just being friendly, but I minded the lack of privacy and sometimes went out of my way to avoid them. When I moved away, the parents feared the snatched thirty seconds with a grumpy daughter would disappear into no contact at all, but in fact I now see them regularly and properly. Meanwhile, the "friendly" parent suddenly gained an interest in subscribing to cable TV soon after I had gone.

The point is, if you can possibly afford to move out, whether renting or buying, it is the best thing you will ever do for your head, if not your bank balance. If it comes down to an either/or scenario, it is absolutely justifiable that your happiness account is healthier than your savings one. Home should provide you some peace of mind, and having parents on top of you 24/7 when you are no longer a child can be a strain on the relationship and lead to regular clashes.

• IDEAL HOME HUNT •

Space always comes at a premium, so figure out what you want from your abode. At this point, you have fewer people and their agendas—whether they be barbecues or phenomenally large high-definition television screens—to consider. As an SG, how much square footage do you really need? Since you are a bachelorette, you can go "French." You are young and free to choose a shabby shoe-box (suitable just for passing out in) with the perfect location, rather than somewhere that involves large **Cabbage** (taxi-cab) fares and several empty rooms.

I've lived in my shoebox for over three years, since at the moment my primary requirement is location, not largeness. In my SG's world, a good home is where buses, the subway, shops of all description, and my working world are right outside my door. I have my own double bed and bathroom and a fridge for keeping alcohol and an old lemon in (great in hot water for detoxing, or for adding to Gin & Tonics when you're back in retox mode).

There's no pressure to be a domestic goddess, as there's literally not enough room. I don't possess an ironing board—there is nowhere to put one. I therefore own a lot of lycra-based clothes and, if need be, place crumpled items in the dryer with a wet flannel for five to ten minutes, which is just as good. I also don't know how to turn on my oven, a fact my mother let slip to my grandmother. It took several moments to recover her celebrated composure at news of this particular granddaughter's ineptitude (my younger, recently married female cousin, in contrast, has a large eat-in kitchen). However, I am an expert microwaver, and if anyone comes to dinner, we go to the pizza place downstairs.

If "feeding the five thousand" makes you happy, you can opt for somewhere larger, although you may also have to purchase hiking boots to get to the bus or train stop. You may want a wreck to restore, or a flawless flat. The important thing is that you feel that your home is your refuge, a place that can rejuvenate you in some way. Rejuvenation has its costs, though, which is why you'll then need to see if you can afford a place on your own, or whether you need a roommate.

• CAN YOU BEAR TO SHARE? •

I have had three roommates, and although I loved them all dearly, they were no good for my mental health, as I am sure I was dreadful for theirs. I spend so much time having to be "on" when I'm out that I cannot possibly face having a conversation when I am in my apartment. This meant my roommates a) got worried about me and never ceased asking if I was all right—very sweet, but very dull having to assure them that I was; or b) were affronted. It was nothing to do with them. I was just all talked out.

Whether or not you share may be a matter of penny-watching instead of personal choice. I've worn my coat indoors to cut down on heating bills rather than put up with a roommate who could share the expense but mutter about the extravagance. Conversely, one of my SG friends was accused by her ex-roommate of being exorbitant for buying non-economy toilet roll, which led to a shouting match about absorbency. However, if you are in the fortunate position of being able to choose, pause and consider your situation. You're no longer a student, when living with people is an essential part of the whole college/university experience. You're out in the real world. Being able to walk around naked, eat what you want, and mess up the bathroom as much as you like are all perks of being single that no one should be deprived of.

One of the major advantages of my minuscule apartment is that there is physically no room for a roommate. No one ever asks, and I have no need to say no. One SG friend who has a second room admits its existence can be a trial at times. People keep trying to move in or stay with her and then take mortal offense when she turns them down, even if they offer her astronomical rent. She works hard for her space and refuses to be swayed by pledges of home-made choc-olate-chip cookies or a ready-made cleaning person on site. Offers of a weekly back massage almost weakened her stance, but she held her ground.

Other SGs I know eschew people for pets. However, consider carefully before getting a live furry friend. A cat may be the traditional accessory for the SG, but in reality they require some attention. I deeply miss my feline, Smirnoff, but not his path of night-time destruction that greeted me every morning. The neighbors also now don't have to worry whether I'm alcoholic, as I'm not squealing out the name of a vodka brand at breakfast-time because my keys had ended up embedded in his litter tray for the umpteenth time. Remember, being an SG is about reveling in your lack of responsibility, not taking it on. Mini-canines may well be the accessories *du jour* for the Paris Hiltons of this world, but these four-legged prima donnas are yours for life, and you probably don't have an entourage to poop-scoop for you. At least a human being living with you is (should be) toilet-trained.

Of course, for some, having other people pottering around is necessary for their sanity. One SG I know cannot live on her own and needs her girlfriends to watch *The OC* with when she has a rare quiet night in. On the other hand, she cannot comprehend my need for utter solitude when I do the same. Whatever your reason for sharing, there are certain pitfalls to avoid, but as long as you are aware of them, you get to share in single life with playmates in tow.

The advantage at this stage of your life is you (finally) get a say in who you live with. When picking a roommate, think about whether you really are compatible cohabiting companions, both financially and personally. I could never live with my BF, despite the panic induced if she is out of **Radio Contact** with me for more than a few hours at a time. Financially my BF is out of my league. She's earning far more than I am and can spend more on everything. Our supermarket trips together would by and of themselves put a huge strain on our friendship. She's also the messiest, laziest, least domesticated person I know. Her dishwasher has been unplugged for over a year (at least the oven I never use is wired up). She just hasn't got around to getting it installed, despite pleas from her long-suffering cleaner. We both know we would be utterly incompatible roommates, but our relationship is secure enough to be able to say that to each other. I do not ever want our friendship to be threatened over who's taken out the trash—she is far too important to me for that.

Several friends of mine love sharing with roommates they never see. Be wary, however, of living with a friend who has a boyfriend. Couples make out on the sofa when you want to watch *The Princess Bride*, or have noisy sex when you need a nap. Even the nicest other halves are irritating when you have to talk to them in your pajamas on a Saturday morning, or scrape their pubic hair off the bath. They are essentially one extra body in a space that cannot accommodate them. Boyfriend creatures are also male. They will have opinions, which they opine, on anything from the cable channel they watch and you pay for, to your love life, your eating habits, or your car. If you do end up an unwitting gooseberry in an unwanted *ménage à trois*, encourage your roommate to spend a lot of time at his place. If you have to resort to wearing skimpy nightwear at all hours around the apartment so she gets slightly concerned about where his eyes are focused, well, sometimes such desperate measures are called for.

Having roommates is all about boundaries; and if you are clear from the beginning what counts as a breach of these—including the amount of time boyfriends, present and future, can stay for—domestic delight can still be yours.

• THE SEARCH •

Now it's time to search for your place, whether it be online, through the classified ads, or via real estate agents or brokers. A note here: you are an SG, so keep safety at the forefront of your mind. If you feel remotely uneasy about viewing anything on your own, phone a friend to come along with you. A companion might even be useful: my GBF once prevented me from buying a place by pointing out that it had no storage space for my shoes (I'd gotten too carried away by the shiny power shower). If you're using a broker, contact the ones in the appropriate area and give them your requirements. Agents and brokers, whether you are buying or renting, need to be managed, exactly like everyone you will ever come across, and dealing with them is purely a matter of common sense.

First of all, network. Meet as many agents and brokers as you can. Charm them, so that if you are buying, they are less likely to let their clients cheat you. I got my shoebox apartment because the agent called me when the previous buyer had dropped out. He also stopped another person with a higher last-minute offer by convincing his client I was the more reliable buyer. Despite their reputation, real estate agents are surprisingly human and respond predictably well to buttering up. Being charming works.

Of course, never speak to them without a CL. The CL will be made up of all the things you want and need your home to be, as well as important questions like: "Who looks after the communal areas? How much is the service charge? Is it true they are planning to re-route a freeway via the front door?" After a few viewings, you'll know your condos from your co-ops.

Buying on your own can do damage enough to your savings, but surveyors' and lawyers' fees can rub serious salt into the wound. Select these people the way you'd select your doctors. Do your research, and, if you can, ask your friends for recommendations. Both these professions will charge the earth to communicate with you in confusing language, so contrast and compare and make sure that you are at least getting the best deal. And if it turns out you cannot afford to get on the property ladder for now, remember—household happiness is about finding a haven to sleep stress-free in.

Don't forget to bribe friends and relatives to help you pack and move. There is a reason why moving house is considered one of the most stressful things you will ever do. However, the years of peace it should bring you afterward, not to mention the toned arm muscles from all that carrying and lifting, should make it more than worthwhile.

• YOUR SET-UP •

So you have the keys, a floor filled with boxes, and a fairly blank canvas. As an SG, you can now do whatever you like. You can take forever to unpack, decorate as you see fit—the only opinion that matters is your own.

Home improvements may be the most boring tasks imaginable to you (I certainly think so), but remember that your home is your sanctuary. The possibilities when it comes to decorating your dwelling are truly endless. One acquaintance has gone for a pink theme—everything from walls to sofas to fridges is, to one degree or another, pink. The pinkwash is perhaps a reaction to her ex-boyfriend, who previously insisted that all interior decoration in their abode be brown, or sewage-colored. He was a complete turd to her too; in that relationship's case, the writing was very much on the s★★t-colored walls.

The renovations needn't cost you a lot of money, either. I have a pal who spent a year doing up her place on a restricted budget, but she still somehow managed to fill it with shiny fittings, along with white sofas, which small hands won't stain. Another SG friend has shoes and pashminas in place of adornments, and her BF makes features out of coats to brighten up her studio apartment—who needs a painting when you can have a DVF dress coat costing just as much as an imitation Pollock on your wall?

It is a myth that girls do not like gadgets, gigantic televisions, and sound systems—however, we know it's perfectly fine not to possess an encyclopedic knowledge of the ins and outs of electronics. Because of this, salesmen may consequently see you, the SG, as a soft touch. If you think you will need an expert when out purchasing such items, phone a friend, although pick your authority carefully. I made the mistake of taking my music producer brother shopping with me for these appliances, since I thought his knowledge would mean I would not overpay. We ended up having a war of words, as he was trying to convince me to buy a TV that would not have fitted in my flat, let alone through the door into it.

A note here: Measure your doorways before buying beds and sofas.

I have had more than one chum unable to get their "no refunds" king-size bed into their new bedroom. The female of the species do not need to give the male any extra ammunition on our so-called inability to think practically. Just because our spatial-awareness skills may occasionally be less than stellar, that does not mean we are unable to survive without a man and his measuring tape (something an SG should always own anyway, although men for some reason fear us possessing one—can't think why).

Since your home is your private place, especially if you do not have to share, it can be a mess or an utter tribute to good taste. You can take along your friends when houseware shopping and ask their opinions, but what works for them may not work for you. This is almost always about your private, not your public, persona. If you don't have enough cups and sometimes end up using a jug as a mug, as your humble authoress has done on occasion, who is to know or care?

Considering you are an SG and undoubtedly out and about most days and evenings, the most critical place in your residence is your boudoir. This is the room where you will spend most of your time, although admittedly the majority of it will be while asleep. The luxury of not having to wage duvet war with a partner and being able to fully stretch out over a double bed with a mattress bounce of your choice may well become a savored memory in later years, so treat this opportunity with respect. Blow your budget and a lot of shopping hours on your bed; it is the most vital thing you will buy. Mine is my most expensive piece of furniture, and I was somewhat embarrassed when I bumped into a skinflint friend of mine while I was purchasing it. My credit card was having problems going through because it cost so much, and I was terrified she would comment on my extravagance (she has been known to bring a calculator to dinner and quibble over who had bread or not). However, she said nothing, which I initially put down to her being caught out in a very unfortunate pair of shorts. When I went round to her place some months later, I found out why. Her bed was a more expensive version of mine. Rest assured, where you lay your head is a sensible expenditure.

Your boudoir needs to be somewhere you can sleep, and thus it is preferable to keep it peaceful, muted, calm—in color, decoration, and vibe. Yet it's also somewhere to seduce; we may be single, but that does not mean we have to live like Maria before she met Captain Von Trapp.

It is a rookie mistake to go back to his place before you have reached the bringing-over-of-a-change-of-clothes stage. Although the sexual revolution has changed many attitudes, the walk of shame is still just that for a female—that panda-eye, bed-hair, evening-outfit look on the trudge to the early morning train or, worse still, at work, is simply not a good one. Since a similar journey is still perceived as the strut of pride for a male, if someone wants to "**kiss**" you, he should make the effort to come back to your place. You therefore need to feel happy and confident in your bedroom. The sex you have in there will register that much higher on the Richter scale for it.

I always have a better time in the boudoir if I have boy-proofed myself and my flat. If a boy is in your bed, you'll probably have had some advance warning. You'll have your body smooth, all embarrassing products such as depilatory cream hidden from display in the bathroom, and neither grey bras nor granny knickers anywhere in sight in your bedroom. However, life does not always go according to plan, and sometimes you will not have had time to order your habitat. No man I have ever met really minds the empty tit-tape and control-top tights packets strewn over the floor. Their mind is on something else entirely. The second time I was "kissing" a certain bachelor in my bedroom, he remarked how unrecognizable it was compared to the bomb site it had been first time round. The mess had not put him off coming back for more, but on this occasion I had a less inhibited experience, with skin more baby- than bear-like and all such paraphernalia out of sight.

If you can afford a cleaning lady, do not be ashamed nor be an inverse snob about having one. Two hours a week helping keep your haven habitable will change your life. You are single, you work hard, and you do not always have time to dust the doorknobs. Several of my girlfriends who work very scary hours have never even met their cleaners. Since I often work from home, I know all about the traumas caused by my cleaner's agoraphobia (fear of crowds), acrophobia (heights), and amathophobia (dust).

Always buy Christmas presents and leave cash bonuses for cleaning ladies. As for all circumstances when parting with cash, get personal recommendations for these domestic goddesses, and try not to be like an extremely anal acquaintance of mine who has been known to utter "Got to go—I have to clean up before the cleaner arrives." Of course, never leave a pigsty for your cleaner, but it's OK to leave them something to do.

• CARS •

The other massive expenditure in your life, other than your abode, may well be sitting outside it. If you have a car, it will doubtless be your second home, with almost as much make-up and SG clutter in it as your stationary one. Make sure, though, you do your calculations carefully to ensure you're making the most of your car. One acquaintance sold her ever-depreciating-in-value-and-increasing-in-expenditure vehicle and now, if she needs to get out of town, hires fun cars that she could never afford to buy. She has turned up in a flashy Ferrari at a very dull wedding, and a luxurious Lotus at a college reunion. This caused all the males, especially those who had bred and were now confined forevermore to large functional vehicles, almost to pass out with jealousy. If a car is going to give you more freedom than grief, and you have the cash, then absolutely buy one . . . but get a license first. I know car owners who have not (seriously).

Once armed with a license, don't worry if you have a general lack of knowledge about automobiles. You will soon pick up what you need to know about things on four wheels, and it is actually extremely cool not to recognize your Mercedes from your Mini Coopers. One boy acquaintance bought an Aston Martin DB7 for six figures. Two different girls in the space of twenty-four hours genuinely complimented him on his new Ford Probe. He sold the Aston at a massive loss soon afterward, this particular vanity project not providing the James Bond pulling power he had hoped.

If you are going to buy a car, the steps that you need to take are exactly the same as dealing with anyone else you require a service from. Research the best places to purchase, and cross-check your findings with friends. It is probably best to buy second-hand, even if only by a few months, as nothing loses value quicker than an automobile. Don't talk with a dealer (and then preferably one outside town—they tend to offer better prices) until you're armed with a CL comprised of questions gleaned from the Net and friends in the know. Consult more than one vendor so you can make an informed decision. It has been proven that women pay more for cars than men do, which is distinctly unfair, so when you buy, take a **Wingman** with you. All these rules apply when servicing and selling too.

This is your chance, again, to get what you want within your budget. You do not have to squeeze in squealing toddlers, sulky teenagers, or stout spouses. Who said a customized pink Mini Cooper wasn't a rational choice for the road? You have the rest of your life to be sensible. If it is your lifetime ambition to own a convertible, and your bank balance says you can afford one, then why not? If you want extra lipstick mirrors that light up (best *not* while in motion, please, SGs), or to opt for a better looking dashboard, then it is your prerogative. You are also allowed GPS. You're perfectly capable of reading a map, or willing to ask people for directions (unlike the male species), but it just may not always be safe to stop and ask.

Too many gadgets, however, can be distracting. I know an SG who bought a device to help with her parking, but when it went off to indicate she was too close to the car behind, she thought it was her cell phone ringing and ignored it. There was an expensive fender-bender. It is a cliché that girls cannot park, and admittedly, one I and my gadget-loving friend live up to, but my mother is the best parker I know (which irritated my ex-stepfather hugely). It is a proven fact, backed up by insurance companies who would never do anything to risk their profits, that women are superior, safer drivers. We have better judgement. One could say we're experts at driving. That and the topic of families, though of course everyone is an expert on relatives—other peoples', that is.

HOME MANAGEMENT

Survival Tips

- As soon as you can afford it, move out of your parents' home. It will make you happy.
- If your priority is location and Cabbage accessibility, then you're free to live in a shoebox, where the only oven you'll have room for is a microwave.
- If you must have a roommate, pick one carefully. Set comprehensive ground rules before leases are signed.
- A cleaning person could change your life: consider employing one.

CHAPTER 4

Family Management

*T*HERE IS A wise old Chinese saying: "Govern a family as you would cook a small fish—very gently." We can all comment with great insight on those we read about in *People*, tut-tutting over a film star's exploits with the nanny, and we will provide a shrewd perspective for our acquaintances on how they should interact with their relatives. When it comes to our own family, however, it will almost always be a different story.

The subtlety and sensitivity everyone needs when managing their worlds is never more vital than in their dealings with family. This is especially true for SGs. For every SG I know, family is the cornerstone of their very being, especially since they have no partner or child to take that role. These are the most complex set of relationships they have to cope with. Family makes them laugh—and cry—harder than anyone else in their SG world. All of my SG friends and I have found it impossible to get it right with our relatives all of the time, especially in the twenty-first century, when multiple sets of families abound (courtesy of a divorce rate at almost one in two.)

• "RELATIVE" VALUES •

The SG has her own specific challenges when it comes to kith and kin. Because she is single, there's the perception she's in a semi-childlike twilight zone. In the past, you became an adult when you got married and had children; otherwise you were a spinster and a burden. Children may now lose their innocence earlier, but they also tend to be in school and single longer—so when do they become adult? The SG generation is something new for society to deal with, so there is no reason for our families to know how to treat us. There are manuals on diaper changing and rebellious teenagers, not on how to deal with an SG living and loving her lifestyle.

Having an available daughter of marriageable age is traditionally a worry for her mother and father. In the back of parents' minds, programmed throughout the centuries, is the thought that as long as she's still single, such a daughter cannot possibly be fulfilled. Until you come to grips with your relatives' concern about your SG status, it may mean you are still considered in childlike terms and are thus on the receiving end of that much more "advice" than attached family members of a similar age.

If you are anything like my SG friends, your familial relations bear more resemblance to the Simpsons than the Partridges. Blood relatives seem all too liable to take offense when none is meant. One SG wept buckets after her graphic designer dad thought it hilarious to mock up an alternative poster of the film Single White Female by substituting her picture for Bridget Fonda's, changing the title to Single Woman Failure.

Neither party in this state of affairs was acting like a grown-up; however, for SGs in particular, it is only natural to want family approval. You love them more than anything, and so their opinions matter more than anyone's. All your family wants is for you to be happy. Unfortunately, nobody is going to be completely happy all the time. The best anyone can hope for is mostly happy most of the time. As an SG, your relatives will worry that you are intrinsically unhappy, and the situation will become a vicious circle, since the burden of their concern will be making you downcast too. The time has come for the SG to manage the troops away from the beltway and back onto the straight and narrow of a Roman Road. Wearing an elegant Russell Crowe-esque skirt, naturally.

• MANAGE EXPECTATIONS •

The first fundamental step in good family management is to handle your relatives' expectations effectively. Leaving home is a giant leap toward an adult relationship with the parents, but you must also leave the Miss Goody Two Shoes act behind too, along with the boy band posters and matching duvet. An SG friend of mine always cleans the kitchen before anyone wakes on a Sunday morning when she visits the parental household. She's never gotten a "thank you," but when her brother did it once, he got the iPod he had been lusting after.

You may find that sometimes your family will try to be indirect when trying to place responsibility on you, but their methods will usually be about as subtle as a sledgehammer. The same SG's father once called her at her office to ask if she thought her irresponsible brother could bake a cake for their mother's birthday. This was an obvious ploy to guilt-trip a girl who works 24/7 into making it. She did, but seethed at the tactic. If her dad had just come out and asked her, she would have happily done so. Instead, there was a pointless ten-minute conversation in the middle of a manic working day when she was just wound up by how she always had to pick up the pieces for everyone else.

I am not advocating becoming a lazy and insensitive person, but if your relatives are running you ragged, insert some boundaries. The more you accept your family's guilt trips, the more of them you'll be subjected to. The hapless SGs end up feeling deserving of the doghouse, while their relatives convince themselves they are so neglected that they are one paw away from an animal shelter. Therefore to become a happy SG, you may have to acknowledge that you will never wholly please your family, in particular your parents. Many of my friends find their relatives contrary at times. If they are successful in their career, they're "working too hard;" if they're not, then they're "a disappointment." Because they don't have a boyfriend, there is the fear, sometimes voiced but continually implied, that they've been "left on the shelf." It'll thus be too late to have babies (never mind that they might not actually want them). Of course, whenever they did have a boyfriend, there was something wrong with him . . . once you have come to terms with the fact that it's impossible to completely—or at least consistently—delight them, life—and family guilt—becomes a lot easier to bear. Make your interactions with your relatives work better for you and, although they may not always realize at the time, for them as well.

I've said earlier that being indirect in areas such as your working world can reap rewards. That's not the case with your family. Because you're an SG, they may regard you as being more at their beck and call than any attached or unreliable (male) relatives. You may need to train your families to actually ask for what they want by ignoring any veiled requests and refusing to act until they spell out exactly what they want. Your family may then consider more carefully whether it is really reasonable for you to be carrying out certain duties, and whether someone else should be pulling their weight instead. What's more, you'll know exactly what help they want. One SG I know was driven to distraction by her grandmother, who had just had a fall, because of the mixed messages her Granny sent about how she wanted the aftercare structured. Because they never had a transparent relationship, every entreaty was hidden in some way. Her grand-mother would have preferred to be in her own home recuperating and watching Tyra Banks in peace, rather than at her cousin's, who only allows Oprah to grace her screen. Emotional guilt-tripping serves no one. It only builds unhealthy resentment. A family full of surface quasi-saints results in devilish demeanors lurking underneath.

Friends have found that if they ensure their relatives do not expect too much, they are not such a disappointment. Their achievements are thus a pleasant and appreciated surprise. I know a girl who left Harvard with top honors and tried her hand in a top advertising firm. She gave it all up to become a gardener. Her social mountaineer-ing parents (they are too advanced to be called climbers) could not understand—what was their high-flying daughter, whom they used to boast about to all their friends, doing? Ultimately, the parents tried to muscle their daughter into therapy. What they couldn't understand is that she just happens to like gardening and is far happier than many "professional" people. Eventually, her parents saw she had taken the right path for her, and ever since the environment became the fashionable cause du jour, they wheel her out at all the fundraising events they attend. Many family members cannot tell you that they are proud, but underneath it all, they undoubtedly are.

To return to the issue of establishing boundaries, here's an example from a confidant of mine. This SG spent so much of her time trying to please her parents—about as easy a task as eating a donut without licking your lips—that they distressed and dazed her straight into ther-apy. The therapist helped her see she needed to stop being so affected by their agendas, and her parents in turn realized they needed to leave their loved one to her own devices more often. Her physique and state of mind improved, she got a new job, and the life *she* wanted was back on track, which was all everyone ever wanted to start with. Only by running your SG lives yourselves, and by encouraging your relatives to relinquish that task if they still consider it theirs, will you be at peace. Some older family members may struggle with the concept. After all, they used to wipe your bottom (or got someone they married, paid, or both, to do it), but they need to come to terms with your independence for everyone's sanity.

Of course it's important to listen to your family, but it is just as vital to realize you do not have to accept everything they say any more; you'll need to find a way to make that point to them. One SG friend had an older, married sister who was especially strident in her views about whether she should be an accountant or an actress. The SG was initially upset at the interference, but then took a step back to examine the situation for what it was. SG reminded her older and supposedly wiser sibling that she herself had moved to Amsterdam to run a "café," much to their family's exasperation. She went ahead anyway and married a Dutch merchant b(w)anker whom she met while serving "cake." Big sis, now Mrs. Stay-at-Home, living in a house way out in the country, was forced to bite her tongue.

Family members of your own generation will understand more about where you are coming from and going to than anyone else on this earth. Yet I have seen my friends tie themselves in jealous knots over their siblings' better looks or bigger bank balances. One SG I know cannot accept that her brother will take over the family business and the apartment above the shop when their dad retires. This despite the fact the business is a garage, and as her car insurance company would vouch for, she does not know the difference between reverse and first gear. For her, it's the principle, but the SGs who have found peace with themselves are the ones who have accepted that it is not their siblings' fault if their parents have spent more time or money on them. Resentment is hard to bear and can cause unsightly furrowed brows that can only be fixed by costly cosmetic procedures, draining money better spent on footwear. I would be lost without my rock of a brother. Siblings should be your allies. So make them that way.

You are your own person. Following your family's every word of advice may not make you any happier, yet occasionally bearing some of it in mind can. It is astounding what experts relatives can be in all aspects of your life, if you let them. Sometimes they will be helpful and come up with career-making suggestions. Other times they'll get it completely wrong. Two of mine were bemused that I turned down a British reality TV show—where the producers try to get celebrities on a desert island to get it on—to instead write this book. I hope it was the right decision! Of course, on other occasions, they have been absolutely correct about the path I should follow. It is always unwise to take anyone else's view as gospel, whether they be friend, foe, or relative; at the end of the day it has to be your decision, as you are the one who will have to live with it.

This point in your SG life is about nourishing yourself into flourishing. Some of the decisions you make in life may not be straightforward, but then life itself is about as easy as walking in a straight line in a pair of oversized Louboutins.

• FAMILIAL ENCOUNTERS •

Real-life visits need to be a regular occurrence, but not routine, so relatives are not reduced to an apoplectic state if you change the plan because something vital has cropped up in your SG world. They need to know that just because you do not have a partner and/or child, you do still have responsibilities. One of *your* responsibilities is to help them realize this. The older generations of your family will not be around forever, and while you love them to bits, they shouldn't leave you in bits.

Here are some steps to prevent this. My SG friends have learned the art of backtracking. For example, they offer to visit for a specified period of time. The relatives complain that it is not for long enough. My friends counter by saying they then won't be able to come at all. Finally, the relatives agree to the initial offer. If their families are being utterly unreasonable, then they sometimes fake being sick and don't turn up at all.

Some relatives may see life as a competition, and, be it men, careers, or body weight, they compare you to both themselves and your contemporaries. One SG friend, an ex-anorexic, read in her mother's Christmas round-robin letter how she was pleased to report that, after 30 years of happy marriage, she was still slimmer than both her 20-something, single daughters. Round-robins should be banned. They're like New Year's Resolutions in creating unnecessary pressure to "achieve." Though if they were, it would leave my mum and myself bereft of our annual wine-sharing ritual, where we weep with laughter over the self-applauding anecdotes of the Cathcarts and Worthington-Smiths (pronounced Smythe, don't you know). If you feel your relatives are putting you down in such an unfair and unrefined fashion, consider for a moment why they are lashing out like this. It's more about their shortcomings than yours. The above-mentioned Mrs. Round-Robin was a desperate housewife hysterical about turning 50 and the thought of middle age and its spread. Such criticism, well-meaning or not, should not set you on a depressing downward spiral; hence it is vital that you come to terms with your own body beautiful.

You may find yourself under an occasional (but heart-in-the-right-place) offensive from your family. If you are en route to a scheduled encounter and think you are in danger of undergoing such friendly fire, make sure you have a CL in reserve, with retorts about career, men, and lack of grandchildren at the ready. The CL may not always be necessary, but it might be invaluable if your relatives know how to pick their moments. I have one German confidante who has a perfectly reasonable relationship with her parents until they all get in a car. While squeezed in the back with her two small half-siblings and two over-sized canines, her super-successful stepmother takes control of the wheel and the conversation. Without a CL, my friend inevitably falls to pieces, regressing to pre-pubescent powerlessness as her father sits in the front making supportive noises to his wife. Until their own offspring start going off the rails and take the pressure off her, the CL is the only way my friend has any chance of seizing the conductor's role from her stepmother and orchestrating the conversation to keep her at bay.

Steering a familial encounter toward sweetness and light is a tactic all SGs need to master, and there are some general topics for the CL that should ensure everyone has a convivial time. Catch up on "news," aka gossip, and ask about their own lives, their friends, and your relatives. Relatives, although they often deny it, love "news;" one friend's aunt positively revels in "bad news." You may not know the second cousin they are talking about, but pretend you do and go along with the diversion. Health is also an exceptionally safe topic. They can go on and on about their ailments—and other peoples'—

for hours. When you've diverted as long as you can and the topic turns to you, you may need to edit your contribution to keep things on a positive note. In your career, there is never a crisis, even if you have been fired. It's not unemployment, it's a repositioning. Be wary when revealing the existence of any **Distractions** of the male variety. Relatives can get slightly ahead of themselves and start composing a wedding speech. They could also take it upon themselves to do some more research. One SG friend of mine was "kissing" a chef who worked in a restaurant near the family home. Her father considers himself a "funny guy," so he dined there and sent such cryptic compliments to the chef that he came out to converse with the client. Papa didn't realize until he had almost had a coronary over the number of tattoos the young man had that he had the wrong man.

However content you are, the fundamental problem, in many a relative's eye, is that you're single. Sometimes they'll try to help, with varying degrees of disaster. If they were part of the swinging sixties and seventies generations, they will have misplaced confidence about being on your wavelength. One acquaintance of mine was 21 when her mother sat her down and told her some women make good wives, and some women make good lovers. Had she made up her mind about which one she was going to be? Apparently she could not be both. Her mother, incidentally, had opted to be a lover and assumed the associated complications of having three children, by three different men, on three different continents (although that is where the semblance with Madonna ends). Another spends every conversation with her daughter speculating over whom she might marry, to the extent she goes through a British society magazine's annual list of eligible bachelors with a highlighter pen. Her daughter, who has a burgeoning career as a merchant banker, is only 23 and hardly anywhere near a shelf.

Relatives like to play cupid. This is normally futile, but don't completely dismiss the idea out of hand if you decide you might like a male **Object** to dally with. The love of my life (so far) resulted from my parents sitting me next to the gentleman at dinner. Your friends and family do know you and thus sometimes get it right. Sometimes, though, they don't. One of my BFs in New York was sent on a date set up by both sets of parents with a man whom she instantly realized was gay. They became best friends, and she was there for him when he finally plucked up the courage to come out to his family. Some SGs I know stand accused by their relatives of being too fussy, but of course, not as fussy as the family would be if they brought home an obese wastrel with an IQ of 22. One of my school friends actually brought home such a specimen when her parents became too impossible on the boy topic. They have not asked about her love life since, learning that information is rationed as a reward for good behavior. The more they pry, the less they get, but the less they interfere, the more she may choose to share with them.

Ultimately, you will have to deal with role reversal, and there will come a time when you have to raise awkward issues with your older relatives, even offer them sensible advice. One SG lawyer acquaintance has prevented her somewhat fickle father from entering his fourth marital union without a pre-nup, saving him a considerable sum. Other times you'll take on the carer role. Always do so with kindness. Upstart youngsters telling an older family member, "You need to stop driving, you're a danger to society," will be a massive blow. You could use **Bunbury**'s older, slightly batty relative to approach the problem, claiming that he or she almost ran over a small child, and you seek your family member's counsel on what Bunbury should do to stop the reckless relative from driving. My friends report that this tactic often helps their relatives realize they should take heed and apply the subtle advice to their own situation.

• TASKS •

Since criticizing your family should be your last resort—you don't want to make any of them feel bad—it's important to acknowledge that they like to feel useful. It's the fear they have of becoming a third wheel that can make them misbehave. You may not have supplied children to be fussed over; however, the SG has other ways of making family feel wanted.

Grant your family a purpose by giving them tasks: essential jobs that they want to do and you either do not, or cannot do. Even though they may mention your shortcomings in not being able to carry out the duty on your own, they will complete the chore for you. These could include sewing, home improvements, car advice, and nursing you through ill health. You can also borrow things from them. Grandparents have useful stockpiles of things like wheelie suitcases in every conceivable size—baggage that you actually want them to give you.

Your family can—and wants to—be a vital support in your hour of need, so let them. I went to hospital to have laser eye surgery and had to allocate aftercare to a parent (there was even a competition over which one would get to look after me—parents can be great!). I chose my Mum, and she luxuriated in the fact that she was needed and spent several weeks arranging my post-op recovery. I was whisked back to my apartment, given a beautiful bouquet of flowers, had my eye drops applied, was tucked up in bed, and had regular calls as to my well-being for weeks. I felt very much loved. And so, I suspect, did she.

Now, if I am ditched, the first person I call is my father. He promptly takes me out to dinner *à deux* and gazes at me adoringly across the table, unable to comprehend how any man could not love me. While this has caused some less salubrious, not to mention slack, hacks to speculate he has a new "mystery blonde" in his life (perhaps my hair color expenditure has been a little high lately), there's nothing like a father's adoration at this low SG point. No man will ever love me as much or think I am as beautiful as my dad does, and many SGs I have spoken to feel the same way.

If you have family members who, for whatever reason, find themselves alone, arrange to do fun things with them, while encouraging them to build up a support network of their own friends. You are their relative, not their best bud. One SG friend's mother was deserted by her stepfather. After ensuring everyone got a fair deal with the minimum use of lawyers, the SG set about schooling her mom in the SG ropes. The daughter rarely agreed to rendezvous with her mom at home for close to two years. Instead, she helped rebuild the shattered older woman's confidence by luring her out to increasingly glamorous places, so she was compelled to leave the house and get dressed up. When they went on vacation together, it was for makeovers on spa breaks. The tough love worked. The much happier pupil now outspends the mistress on shoes and has just as hectic a social life. Mother and daughter even both recently bumped into each other in a nightclub and were eyed up by the same group of 25-year-old males. Mummy even had a rather yummy time with one of them.

With a little management, a healthy and happy relationship with every member of your family can be yours. You do love each other, and even though your patience will be tried repeatedly, it would be a heartbreaking loss if you avoided each other so long that you regretted it in the end. Nowhere will this be more evident than the holiday season, which for so many is anything but jolly.

• THE HOLIDAY SEASON SURVIVAL SECTION •

More people end up in divorce lawyers' offices in January than at any other time of the year, and with good reason. Whether it be Christmas or Hanukkah (or indeed *The OC*'s Seth's Chrismukkah), followed by New Year's Eve, for some families the holiday season can be a seriously challenging experience. Human beings are contrary souls, and if it is compulsory to have a good time, we invariably do not. Add to this having to spend time with people you don't normally choose to play with. If you love the festive season, feel free to skip this section, but most people have traumas dealing with their families. This is especially true for SGs, who are crammed into single beds at familial homes and are given mournful looks because they have not supplied the proceedings with over-tired, obnoxious brats to give everyone an earache. But here's a happy thought, even if you are allocated a 5' x 2' bed when you visit. You don't have any in-laws and thus are not multiplying the amount of family management needed. A mother-in-law, so I understand, can be the ultimate nightmare.

The problem with Christmas for SGs is that it is all about family and children. The family she has are probably indulging in toddler-like tantrums, while she will have no pipsqueaks of her own demanding mom join in the excitement about how Santa drank all the whisky left out for him. Although Rudolph the reindeer seemed to be off his carrots . . . Compounding the situation is that the SG has reached a stage in life where her relatives have had at least two decades to nurture an obsession with tradition that can scale quite scary proportions. There is a routine that must be adhered to, and if it is broken, mass offense occurs. I know of one father who sulks if everyone is not up by 7.30, in church by 8.30, and in front of the Queen's Christmas broadcast by 3—and heaven forbid if anyone opens a present before lunch. Of course, he does not actually do any of the wrapping or present buying, although he does make a great show of using every pan in the kitchen to make the bread sauce, while everyone around him reaches boiling point at his rigid behavior.

Does it really matter if you open all your presents before breakfast or make gravy from a packet? Of course not, so fight back. Once you hit adulthood, suggest breaking with tradition, whether it's moving Christmas dinner to a restaurant or spending Yuletide out of the country. The ultimate break with tradition is to not show up at all. This may put everyone's noses out of joint, but it's also by far the best option for the SG. Your stiletto boots were made for walking (well, taking very small steps to the nearest Cabbage) and will be wasted on the company of people force-feeding you Cruciferae. Why do you have to spend Christmas freezing in a cramped space alongside grumpy souls? Being single means being able to think outside the box. Spending Christmas with your friends—the family you choose—is becoming an important milestone to adulthood. You love your family, you make the effort to spend quality time with them the rest of the year, but Christmas is the only time when the majority of your work stops. Take advantage of the break. A friend who runs her own advertising business can only get away during Christmas. Her mother has been trained to cope without her at Christmas and to make the most of spa weekends with her daughter the rest of the year.

When my BF and I were 25, we both had a very tough year that culminated in the pair of us being ditched by men we had really loved. Neither of us could face a Christmas looking at the endless Public Displays of Affection of our attached younger relatives. So we escaped to a remote cottage where the only cell phone reception to be found was up on a sand dune, on which we precariously balanced to phone various homes on Christmas day. I will never forget skipping along the beach after we had watched *Ferris Bueller's Day Off* and feasted on salmon (for me) and steak (for her), feeling more than a little superior at the sight of all the sullen families around us. We returned revitalized and refreshed, and our unexpected presence at family Christmases ever since has been that much more appreciated.

You may also choose to spend Christmas alone. Christmas is an event for people who do not go out as much as your average SG. My single friends I often find ourselves out every night of the week, partly for work, and partly for fun. In December, excursions become especially intensive for the single soul, so by the holy day itself, you're all talked out. One SG friend literally can't speak to anyone by this stage; she invariably so over-does her activities during the festive season that by Christmas she has lost her voice and is usually bed-ridden with bronchitis for most of it.

If you do decide to **Not F**king Invite (NFI)** *anyone* on Christmas, you may have to be very determined, nay stubborn, to get away with it, perhaps even resorting to telling everyone you are spending it with Bunbury. Alternatively, I have several friends who work for charities over Christmas. No one should ever behave so badly as to complain about someone's absence for this reason. If they do, they can be firmly and swiftly put in their place.

Part of the problem of absconding from Christmas is that relatives can interpret this as a gesture of you not valuing them. You do. Give plenty of advance notice, then hold your nerve. You are not destroying the family unit. You might even suggest that everyone else also goes away on holiday. They may begrudgingly thank you for it come January. Ignore the woeful comments about your impending absence ("Who will untangle the Christmas lights now?"). Instead, counter each negative comment with a happy one: "It's so great you're being so understanding about me going away, not like Bunbury's relatives; it makes such a difference us having such an adult relationship," etc., etc. Finally, arrange to see your family properly another time in January when there is nothing (and nobody) to do anyway, and when the mood destroyers alcohol and caffeine are not so prevalent. Make sure you send them really good presents, although gifts are, of course, another minefield, especially for the SG, who can't share either their cost or location labor. Not for nothing is Santa an anagram for Satan. The legendary fight between Van Gogh and fellow painter Gauguin, during which the former sliced off his ear and gave it to a lady friend, took place at Christmas. At least your unwanted presents are never *that* bad.

There are some silver linings for the SG in the Christmas clouds. You will not have to share gifts with a partner or an entire family, even if all you receive is a hamper containing such gastronomic delights as cherry brandy and blue cheese mayonnaise. However, to make sure you really reap the benefits of receiving your own present, implement present lists. Exchange them with your relatives. Maintain a Christmas book in which every year you note down what you have given everyone so there is never any (unplanned) present repetition. The Internet is your friend. Most of my SG friends now do 80 percent of their shopping online. It involves minimum effort and maximum amount of tea drinking (or coffee drinking in America). They also now give better gifts and blow less better-spent-on-clutch-bags cash, because they can calmly think about what to buy, rather than getting furious in crowds and making rash, extravagant selections. And order early, in November, not in December, when packages tend to get delayed. This will cause you to arrive present-less, which will then cause the little ones to start sobbing.

Keep your own "present list" to useful things that relatives know how to purchase, like saucepans and suitcases, and that cannot be used as ammunition against your SG lifestyle. Requests for sex shop gift certificates, even if they are bestowed, will no doubt be sniped about while the turkey (the most boring meat in existence) has to go back into the oven for another three hours because it is still as bloody as everyone's moods. You can never be too specific about what you ask for for Christmas. One friend of mine requested a small black umbrella, as she was always losing hers. She got one, albeit with "interesting" patterns. She still has the umbrella, but would rather go Miss Wet T-shirt in front of a building site than use the unsightly thing.

On receiving presents, never raise your hopes too high, and develop a thick skin against any perceived SG slights. One daughter I know received in three successive years as her only presents from her frugal mother: a grunge-colored wash cloth, an orange plastic bookend, and then, when the younger woman had been recently ditched by her long-term partner, a teapot-for-one so tiny it would not even provide a small cuppa.

For those SGs who feel reluctant but duty-bound to attend the family Christmas, acquire a bunker mentality. You only have to do this once a year. My SG posse are exponents of the survival strategies of both amused detachment and taking perverse pleasure in any hideousness that might arise. If you are really concerned about how it will go, strictly limit the time you spend *en famille*—arrive late, leave early, and if possible drive, so you have an escape pod. And encourage random people to attend. They're invaluable—they tend to act as a buffer and make everyone behave better and not regress to childhood stereotypes, though consider carefully whom you invite. One girlfriend of mine who had finally, on her 30th birthday (which falls at Christmas), convinced her family to break with convention and spend the holiday abroad in Morocco, brought along a school friend, who had known the family since she was 11. The friend decided to bed her host's little brother, and they spent the trip holding hands and having noisy sex, keeping everyone in their villa awake.

It's prudent for you to prepare a lengthy CL for the duration and, again, purchase good presents. I am the Christmas stocking queen, making sure all females in the family get fabulous ones. Keep everyone's alcohol consumption, including yours, sufficient to take the edge off—a calming buzz, if you will. This will allow you to block out anything you do not want to hear. Take charge of handing around the canapés if you want to reduce the time spent actually conversing, and encourage excursions, even if they are only to the local store. Selflessly lose at board games if you can possibly manage it. From your friends' texts, you know (unless they went away) that no one is having a better time than you.

Then go home, write your thank you letters, and use any remaining limit on your credit card to pre-book your trip to somewhere far away from it all next year. Family can usually be managed, and your relationship can be a good one, but Christmas can test the skills of any expert. Mercifully, you have two families—the one you're born into, and the one you choose. Your friends.

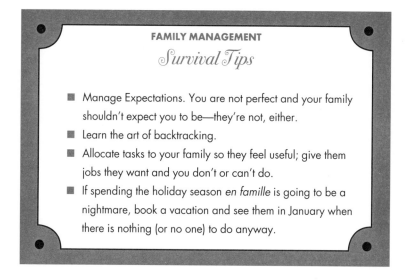

FAMILY MANAGEMENT

Survival Tips

- Manage Expectations. You are not perfect and your family shouldn't expect you to be—they're not, either.
- Learn the art of backtracking.
- Allocate tasks to your family so they feel useful; give them jobs they want and you don't or can't do.
- If spending the holiday season *en famille* is going to be a nightmare, book a vacation and see them in January when there is nothing (or no one) to do anyway.

CHAPTER 5

Friend Management

RIENDS ARE AN essential part of balanced living and being, especially when you are single. They are the family you get to pick; your playmates when you want to have fun, your support network when you're down, your helpers who'll pick up a screwdriver when you need to assemble a bookshelf, and will also pick up their virtual tools whenever your heart's in need of fixing. Unlike lovers, who can so often be the cause of problems to begin with, your friends are not going to desert you in times of distress. Nurture them; since you're single, you have the time to lavish attention on your friends. I have lost count of the number of couples I know who lead such insular lives that, when their relationships imploded, they had to rebuild their network of friends because they'd neglected them *so* when they were an "us."

Bona fide confidants will not only be there for you when bosses, doctors, men, and relatives are pushing you over the edge, but they will offer you assistance when you least expect it and when you need their help the most. One SG found herself pulling off a minor miracle in a "feeding-the-five-thousand" fashion for her grandparents' thirtieth anniversary of their pub opening. She thought her grandmother said in her lilting Irish voice that "four to five" of the family's friends, plus the extended clan of traditional Irish proportions, had been invited. Forty-five acquaintances, as well as relatives, were actually guest-listed. The SG's brothers and cousins threatened our SG's entire loaves and fishes routine when, instead of following the FHB (family hold back) rule to make the food last as long as possible, they decided to stack their plates sky high. The party was in danger of a cocktail sausage shortage, but the SG's BF since birth (hence always invited), rescued the situation, rushing out mid-Riverdance to the supermarket. Friends succeed in supporting us because they are that much more in tune with us; their awareness and acknowledgement skills usually superior to that of your kin.

As an SG, it is vital to have in your world people whom you don't have to walk on eggshells with, to whom you can say anything, whose friendship runs so deep with you they'll never judge even your mean and irrational behaviour. There cannot, by definition, be that many eggshell-free friends in your life—this degree of intensity is just too great to sustain with a vast number of people. There are, of course, different types of friends, with varying degrees of closeness. There will be newer friends whom you'll be seeing more of because you're just getting to know them; others you'll closely watch what you say to because of their insecurities. However, you shouldn't resent giving time to your friends; if you do, you need to re-evaluate these peoples' place in your world. Friendships should be voluntary, not compulsory.

To attain maximum enjoyment of your SG life and ensure that it is sufficiently spiced up, it's essential to have an extensive variety of friends on your playlist. The foundation of your SG world will be your **Genuine Girlfriends**. You can say *any*thing to these gorgeous girls, and if you are having a rant, they will either concur with you and join in, or steer you back to the right and reasonable path. You can go out for cocktails with them and be safe in the knowledge that however many you imbibe, the "cock-tales" told will go no further. Furthermore, Genuine Girlfriends faithfully adhere to the "girl's code" of behavior—specifically not "kissing" each other's exes or befriending these men when they should be ostracized.

Some of your Genuine Girlfriends may change along with your circumstances, but there will undoubtedly be constants throughout your life whom you would be lost without, and probably one in particular—your BF. I have known my BF since I was 11, and she knows more about me than I do. She has a grown-up job compared to my fluffy ones, so lives a completely different life from mine. As a result, we rarely see each other, but our outlook on life is the same. We speak at least twice a day, about anything and everything. She understands the way my relatives tick and gives invaluable advice in managing them. She's so in tune with me that I can call her up from a restaurant and ask her what dessert I want and she will tell me.

There is a reason why every legendary fictional SG who appears on the screen or in print (Grace, Bridget, Carrie) has a GBF. If you can find one, he will become more important to your SG's existence than a lung. They are always bitchier, sluttier, and hairier than you are. I have known mine since graduation, and we are inseparable, despite an unfortunate incident on the night we met when, after one too many vodkas, he put me on the wrong night bus to a suburb far outside of London (imagine heading to NYC's East Village and ending up stranded in New Jersey). With my GBF, I can be as impertinent as I like about people in my world and he will be ruder. If I have been naughty with a boy, he will have behaved ten times worse with ten times as many. He will also be unstintingly honest about my looks and has promised to tell me when it's time for me to undergo some procedures.

Much of the SG's life is about the quest for balance, making a **Straight and Male Best Friend (S&MBF)** an eminently helpful companion. The outside world may think you are actually "kissing," or are destined to end up together. One SG friend's parents I know are convinced she's going to marry hers, even though she has more sexual chemistry with her GBF, who spends more time dressed as a "*laydee*" than Tyler Perry does. You have to be very clear about where you stand with your S&MBF, meaning there can be no flirtatious frisson between you two. My S&MBF and I don't fancy each other, but we do love each other like siblings. He's also invaluable in giving good advice from the alien perspective of the straight male (although several gay men I know have hoped to persuade him off his rampantly heterosexual path).

When it comes to playmates, the SG generally has two types to choose from. The first, Girl Playmates, are friends who you wouldn't confide everything to, but are priceless at partying. Because you don't know them that well, you can neither sulk nor be somber in their company. Thus they're invaluable at making you forget your cares so you do stay out for that half a drink more . . .

Then there's the **Platonic Boyfriend (PB)**, a male friend who you do not "kiss," but have a smidgen of sexual tension with. While they're liable to drift away if you get embroiled in a real relationship, I love PBs. They are very useful—they will help with various chores around your apartment, such as helping to move heavy furniture, and will generally run round after you in a way they never would if you slept with them. One of my PBs conveniently has offices ninety seconds from my apartment, so he can be called on at a moment's notice to change light bulbs I cannot reach. He has also visited at 3 a.m. to locate my stopcock for me, without any indecent reference to his anatomy. PBs also can be the best company, since you make each other look good; a proper male/female friendship always intrigues outsiders. Of course, there are almost always moments with this type of friend when you are faced with the suggestion that you "kiss," which I'll deal with later, but remember the moment any sort of bodily fluid is exchanged, he by very definition cannot be your PB any more.

Completing the SG's balanced friendship circle are a variety of "at least I'm not them" friends, who can sympathize with you during moments of crisis, and also help you realize how fortunate your own life is. There's your friend who's attached to such a dreadful boyfriend/husband you thank God you're single. There's also your older and, I hate to be callous, less attractive friend, whom you can sympathize with about misbehaving work colleagues, parents, and men. There's nothing wrong with acknowledging you have less attractive friends as long as you offset them with friends far more beautiful than you. You'd think life's easier for a supermodel type, but if you have one as a friend you know it's not. The most stunning woman I know has the most appalling time with the men in her world. Her latest rake decided to embark on an affair—with her much younger half-sister. Her perfectly measured and reasonable response involved said lecher, some lube, and YouTube.

Finally, never forget the friend every SG needs, and is, almost beyond any other in importance, is: a Bunbury. Bunbury, as mentioned before, is an Oscar Wilde creation from *The Importance of Being Earnest*; your imaginary friend who can provide a convenient excuse about or example for almost anything.

• FINDING FRIENDS •

The trickiest times to meet friends are when you move to somewhere new. Your whole support network is suddenly miles away, and you have to create a new one. I was living in New York in my early 20s and called up my father in tears, suffering the homesickness from hell. He wisely pointed out that while New York can be the most fantastic place in the world, it can also be the loneliest. Although I'm painfully shy (I hide it well), by obeying an all-knowing SG's friend's mantra to "never refuse an invitation," I figured out my way round it.

Happiness will never be yours if you spend your whole time hiding under the duvet; you have to put yourself **in harm's way** to find it. If you're moving somewhere new, ask your friends if they know anyone you can connect with there. Then be ruthless about getting out and meeting them. If this method is not supplying enough potential pals, take up a new activity, be it skydiving or salsa. The Internet may also (sometimes) surprise you with introductions to fabulous new creatures. I once even had a romantic interlude with a man I met online. A Google image search of his name and confirming with mutual friends that he met my minimum height requirement of six foot ensured there were no surprises when we met face-to-face. Always stay skeptical, though. One somewhat spaced-out SG friend was shocked when she met up with a MySpace message man for munchies and found he was not quite the Matthew McConaughey look-alike his profile picture implied. (She believes that because you never know where a new friendship might lead, she aims to keep her latest acquaintances attractive . . .). Fortunately she had taken, on her Genuine Girlfriends' insistence, a karate-kicking friend along as backup.

If you find a new friend via an old one, be careful not to put the introducer's nose out of joint by "friend stealing." Subsequent meet-ups, for a time, must always occur with your introducer present. Remember, life is too short to make enemies because they have taken inadvertent offense at your behavior. I met my GBF via someone we now no longer see, and we were careful to let our relationship develop in her full knowledge and view before quietly losing touch with her. She spent so much time on her CrackBerry that she deserved her gooseberry status anyway.

If you have met new friends through an ex, this code of courtesy doesn't apply. One SG friend met a fabulously fun set of playmates because of a boy she briefly dated. The wife-beater-wearing DJ (he was a combination of every deck-spinner cliché that exists) assumed she would be easily dispensable if things went awry, but what he had not counted on was that she would get along so well with everyone he knew. She went with it, as his good-time-inducing friends were compensation for his very *short* shortcomings. Soon she was guest-listed to yet another wild club night by his promoter pal and exacted the perfect revenge by meeting her next love interest in front of her ex's decks.

• KEEPING FRIENDS •

Whether it's your body, your home, your work, or your parents, these all require maintenance. Your friends are no different; however, should they require more nurturing than you wish to give and do nothing but drain you, you need to reassess your relationship. If someone complains that you haven't called him or her, have they taken the time to call you? It's so easy to make a quick call while tottering between appointments, or to send a one sentence e-mail or one-word text. (A word of warning: if you're texting while crossing the street, look both ways. I was in four-inch heels dressed for a Kylie look-alike contest at a gay bar when I was struck by a bicycle because I was concentrating on my cell. Sadly, my GBF's boyfriend beat me in the "best hot pants" contest—it is so unfair how men get less cellulite than girls).

You are a crazy-busy SG being pulled (and occasionally pulling) in different directions. That doesn't mean you neglect your nearest and dearest. It's not always about physically seeing someone, it's simply about contact. Friendship is about give-and-take. If neither party makes the effort to stay in touch, perhaps it is not a friendship worth keeping.

If you do decide a friend is worth holding onto, stop and think about how the other person feels, and act accordingly. I believe in sending actual letters. Never a long missive, but real bits of paper that involve a stamp, whether it be a birthday or a "men are mean" card. When a girlfriend (or GBF) needs some TLC, these say so much more than an e-mail or text. I also arrange rendezvous, whether for drinks, dinners, movies, or even vacations. Many times these are the things you do on a date, but you don't have to stress about the spot that appeared on your nose that morning.

However, the onus must not be on you to organize everything. I used to run myself ragged arranging reunions for all my school friends, thinking everything would fall apart if I was not on the case. Eventually I got so busy I had to let the others do it. Lo and behold, we all managed to meet up anyway—just in locations I would not have chosen. I then found the time to organize things again, and quit complaining!

In every friendship, there will be awkward moments. It is a relationship, after all, and people are complicated. You may have foibles that get on another's nerves. For instance, some like to divide a restaurant bill exactly, getting a calculator out, infuriating the more easy-going attendees. With such irritations all you can do is not resort to any playground-type behavior. There are more serious occasions when measured confrontation may be called for, such as when you've gained a new friend that you've been spending a lot of time with. New BFs can unsettle old friends, but we all need fresh blood in our circles. If they're feeling insecure, remind them they have a history with you that's irreplaceable. If they complain more, they're being irrational, and you need to tell them so.

• WINGMAN SELECTION •

The term "Wingman" is no longer the exclusive domain of pitiable males working in tandem on two females, when one chats up the "uglier" girl, leaving his friend to go in for the kill with the other. The designation has, quite rightly, been appropriated by the SG. Now, "Wingman" is another expression to add to the older one of "Walker," used to describe the friend you choose to accompany you to events/nights out, etc. It's rare you won't be allowed a "plus one" at a party, and if you're not, that's probably because it's a set-up by whoever is hosting (odd numbers upset placements). It is no mean feat to select the right Wingman for the right occasion. It could be your GBF, a Genuine Girlfriend, or one of your selection of PBs (although there is the danger of getting drunk and sleeping with him—see **Accidental Sex** in Chapter Eight).

The Wingman is your essential accessory for every social occasion. You need to avoid picking someone who will be a Social Hand Grenade and embarrass you in some way, or who will be ill at ease and unable to cope with the event—that would be unfair to both of you. I always take my S&MBF to theater events, where he works the room like a smoldering knife through butter. Once when he was unavailable, I made the mistake of taking one of my other PBs. His handsome self was completely uncomfortable, overwhelmed by a deluge of friends of Dorothy. It was a disservice to both of us I won't be repeating. By the same token, I completely accept that I will not be the person my friends invite camping. I like my running water to involve a faucet and wouldn't be an asset in the wilderness. Think carefully about who's going to be at the event you're going to, how much time you can spend with whomever you're taking, and whether they will manage or malfunction if you have to leave them on their own for a while. They should also have the capacity to **pull the ripcord** for you if they sense you getting too tired and emotional and take you out of an event and safely home (accidents occasionally do happen, and the danger exists that you may sometimes prop up a bar a little too long).

In my experience, gay friends make the best Wingmen. My confirmed bachelor friends are entertaining, and there is never the possibility they will get amorous, leaving you to fend off an awkward lunge at the end of the evening. Chivalry is not dead—it has just been vanquished to the realm of the gay man. The ones I know are far more gallant than any of my straight male friends, who if they offer to walk you home, only bother in the hope of a "kiss." If a gay man offers to escort you back to yours, they do so just because it is the right thing to do.

• IMPOSSIBLE FRIENDS

Everyone has rough patches, and it's essential you're there for a friend who is going through one. You are not a fair-weather or fast friend.

However, there has to be balance for a friendship to work. One girl-friend seems to collect depressive friends. Something in her obviously likes the feeling of being needed, but at the same time they all expect so much from her that she has ended up seeing a counselor herself. Friends have to acknowledge that they need to help themselves. You cannot be their therapist. If they really are in that bad a state, they must see a professional and, if necessary, resort to anti-depressants.

If someone is draining you when you have nothing left to give, there will come a point where you either don't see them for a bit, or you need to tell them what they are doing to you by asking for help you cannot offer. If neither somewhat crushingly candid approach is appealing, try the classic Bunbury tactic. Say that he/she is at her wit's end about a perplexing pal and is about to tell her they either need professional help or to get a life. Or you can claim that it is Bunbury who is causing you the trouble.

There are friends who are bad for you for different reasons. I like alcohol, but I should not drink it to excess because I am in recovery from a thyroid problem. Some friends support me, raising their eyebrows the minute I move toward polishing off a wine bottle. Others surreptitiously fill up my glass. There are friends who are great for dancing until dawn, and/or there are others who enjoy illegal substances, which have never been my thing. If the evening degenerates in this direction, sometimes these friends do not want to hang out with me because they think I'm boring. By the same token, I am always happy to leave at that point. When they hoover cocaine, they're like hurricanes leaving a path of destruction in their wake. This is always beyond tedious for those who aren't high, whom it invariably falls upon to amend the immediate devastation. This is especially true because cokeheads are under the chemical misapprehension that they are the life and soul of the party.

It is only natural that as we age, friends sometimes drift apart. I happen to still be incredibly close to a good number of high school pals, but fewer college ones. To be sure, they're lovely people, but we no longer have anything in common. They're married and safely ensconced in their significantly-square-footaged houses, while I'm out almost every night for work or play. Our compatibility has changed as our priorities have. The difficulty with drifting apart is when you are the first person to realize that you have both outgrown the friendship. As of this writing, my 30th birthday dinner is proving a minefield to negotiate. Several acquaintances will sulk if they're not invited, despite the fact that I haven't corresponded with them in over two years. These friends are all in couples and cannot comprehend why I would possibly NFI their partner whom I've only met once or twice, nor why I complain that my cell's SIM card is too small for the catalogue of numbers I need. I like collecting people, and because I'm out so much, the numbers quickly add up. Also, because I don't cook, I have a lot of take-out restaurants in my phone's address book. Most of these couples seem to stay in, utilizing a strange tome called a recipe book. Indeed, I have a coupled-up friend like this who hardly ever uses her cell phone, while the bill for mine is my biggest expense after shoes.

These attached female types can get irritating; thus the drift occurs. Pre-engagement, they stress about the possibility of a ring and so are always cancelling on you for him. After the wedding they often become boring, and in-between they become . . . Bridezilla. Bridezilla has no idea how uninteresting she is. The adornment on her wedding ring finger is distasteful, her ideas of a bachelorette night hideous, and her giant doily of a wedding dress is almost as unsightly as the proposed flower arrangements she insists on discussing in great detail with you. Of course, your engaged friend may never turn into Bridezilla, and remain lovely throughout. I do know a few of these, but they are not in the majority. Try and spay Bridezilla by setting up a get-together with a mutual friend with toddlers who's starved for adult conversation . . . then don't show up (Bunbury needed you). If she really insists on your involvement in the wedding preparations, pretend you don't like discussing nuptials because they make you feel so alone. It's a lie, of course, but it might shut her up.

The other area where friendships can be sorely tested is when you do business with pals. In some ways, it's almost like "kissing" them—and can often prove the kiss of death to your camaraderie. I have twice made the mistake of mixing the pleasurable and professional. The first arrangement dissolved amicably. We were both women, and when we each realized we could not give the other what she needed, we talked it through and brought in the lawyers late in the day just to resolve the issue officially. The second was tougher, as a man felt I had done him ill, but two of his BFs and my lawyer both said he could not deliver and would screw me over if I continued my association with him.

Occasionally, when a friend turns out to be a nightmare, it may become essential to drop him or her completely. If this happens, just try and let the relationship run its course by straying out of touch rather than having a massive rift with each other. It is always possible to encourage this by not replying to texts or e-mails from them asking if this is still your mobile number or e-mail address . . .

• ENEMIES •

The old adage "Keep your friends close, your enemies closer," is a shrewd one. Estranging people is immensely dangerous, so turn on the killer charm around people you distrust. You are smarter than they are and don't want to give such types ammunition to besmirch your reputation. One SG was driven to distraction by an attached acquaintance who thought she had been flirting with her husband (she hadn't) and who then went around town bad-mouthing her. Only by the SG saying lovely things to all and sundry about Mrs. Nutcase for a lengthy period did it finally dawn on everyone who in actuality was the b★tch.

Then there are the people brought into your world because your friends are dating them. My girlfriends tend to introduce either bastards, who always give good conversation but treat them dreadfully, or nice but dull men. Be pleasant, but don't put yourself out for them if it's obvious they are going to last no longer than an iPod battery. My male friends, who are often thinking even less with their brains, have been known to date women who give the fairer sex a bad name. One playboy of a PB slept his way around London before the tables were turned, with the player himself being played, and by no less than a gold-digger. She had no girlfriends—the worst sign—and had slept with most of his friends before casting her eye on him once she had cast-iron proof his was the biggest . . . bank balance. I made my feelings known to him, then took a step back and let her dig her own grave. I learned long ago to never force a besotted friend to choose between their lover and you. The sex will always win . . . at first. Let them get out of the honeymoon period.

There is another variety of unfortunate girl men are attracted to—the small, squeaky, stupid ones. A **Squeaky** is a "man's woman" rather than a woman's woman, the type who will ignore every girl in the room if there's a boy to flirt with, and who would certainly never abide by the girl's code, "kissing" any man if she thinks it might get her somewhere. They always giggle at the most appalling jokes made by their target, flutter their overly mascaraed eyelashes, eat only half of what they are given—including things like Gummi Bears—and expect men to pay for everything because they have to spend money on essentials like shoes. (Every girl needs shoes, but nice girls will never set out to bankrupt a boy.) One friend ditched her then boyfriend partly because he insisted on hanging out with his best bud and his Squeaky girlfriend every weekend, and both boys held Squeaky in high regard.

I find the best way to really irritate a Squeaky is to monopolize her in an overtly lovely manner when she is in male company. She will be desperate to ditch you for more social mountaineering interaction, but she cannot be rude within a gentleman's earshot. If she is, the little madam is shooting herself in her tippy-toes. If you are stuck on your own, compliment her about her nail varnish/lipstick. She will go on forever about where she found them, and you won't have to make any further conversation with the airhead, freeing you to contemplate serious issues, such as who will win *Dancing with the Stars*.

Of course, if your friends permanently attach themselves to these people, they have to be tolerated. You must also carefully measure what you say if they ask your opinion. If you are honest about their beloved and they marry, it is a disaster . . . then again, if they marry, that may be a disaster in itself. With a divorce rate of almost one in two, for any couple at whatever income level, a pre-nup is something, as a friend, you should be suggesting, especially if there is not much in the bank to go round if it all goes t★ts up.

Whatever you do, it's best not to wait until the wedding to discuss this. Speaking of which, how do you handle an occasion of this magnitude—as well as other potentially perilous events for an SG? Read on . . .

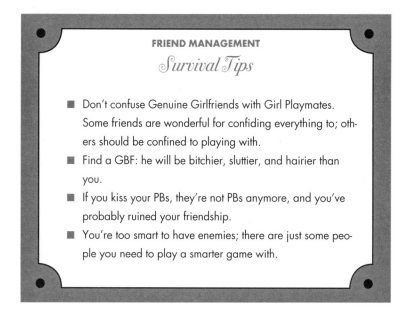

FRIEND MANAGEMENT

Survival Tips

- Don't confuse Genuine Girlfriends with Girl Playmates. Some friends are wonderful for confiding everything to; others should be confined to playing with.
- Find a GBF: he will be bitchier, sluttier, and hairier than you.
- If you kiss your PBs, they're not PBs anymore, and you've probably ruined your friendship.
- You're too smart to have enemies; there are just some people you need to play a smarter game with.

CHAPTER 6

Event Management

*E*VENT MANAGEMENT COVERS practically all your excursions that occur outside of a 100-foot radius of your home. Being out is the oxygen, the very lifeblood of the SG. We're not tied to our abodes by any strings, apron or otherwise, and thus have the opportunity to enjoy ourselves better than any of our contemporaries who are obliged to consider their "better" half. Yet because of the extensive periods we spend outside our households, we are inevitably also more discerning about what fun is. SGs don't waste their time at a soirée they consider substandard when they can easily get to a superior one. There is no need to negotiate an exit with a belligerent boyfriend enthralled with dull discussion and bad beer.

As with work events, you do not have to accept every invitation you receive. Bunbury has the convenient (for you, at least) tendency to require your precious presence at the most crucial moments. Indeed, Bunbury's state of mind may be such that you will only know at the last minute, after your host has given you the exact details of the occasion, whether you will be able to attend, although naturally you may have to rush back to Bunbury at a beeping phone's notice (prime a friend to text/call you). I'm a great believer in attending an event that may not sound promising for at least a short while to discover if you are missing anything. As my grandmother says, you can sleep in your armchair when you're old.

Human beings are, by their very nature, contrary, so if you find yourself trapped in a location and told to have a good time, it's highly likely you won't. Avoid boat parties that actually involve sailing and places where you are unable to get transportation out. I once suffered a torturous evening with an ex-boyfriend on a boat cruising the Thames. He hid until the anchor was raised, wise enough to realize I'd have scarpered back down the gangplank if I'd seen him, then ambushed me, determined to convince me I should forget his infidelity. Salt was rubbed into my wounds still further by the unobstructed view of empty Cabbages with yellow lights whipping down the Embankment, promising escape.

Attending soirées in obscure locations can sometimes be fun, but you should always retain the ability to pull the ripcord if need be. If possible, pre-book a Cabbage, as the more remote the venue, the less such transportation will be available. You can invariably move the collection time to later, or cancel it altogether, if you're having a spectacular time. Knowing there is the option to leave somehow provides a sense of liberating freedom that allows you to revel ever more raucously. It also means your vibe at the end of the evening is not ruined by having to wend a ridiculous route home. My Wingman for a recent foray forgot to pre-book a Cabbage, so I had to walk home at midnight barefoot (the four-inch heels were just too much).

Along with establishing your exit strategy, how much you enjoy the gathering will stem from how well you've managed your expectations prior to it. Some of the fun comes from anticipating an event, but expect too much and it could be a real let-down. Experience dictates that the occasions you expect to be fabulous will habitually not live up to the hype, while those you are somewhat dreading are the most fun. This is why school nights, Sunday to Wednesday ones, are so often the best evenings out. Unlike weekend evenings or Thursdays (which don't count because you only have one work day to get through), there is less buildup, so you can be surprised into having a good time. The minute you bank on having a Sunday morning hangover is when you'll have nothing worse than bed hair, while if you are confirmed for a 7 a.m. Tuesday step class, the sum total of your activity will be hitting your alarm's snooze button. Surprise can lead to such satisfaction.

Now it's time to concentrate on you. To sparkle you have to feel good about yourself, so pull yourself together into a package that will shine, but still be suitable for the event. Your outfit for a sweaty club won't be the same as for your sister's wedding, so think hard as to whether Skechers or stilettos are more suitable. Wear something befitting the occasion, but that maintains your individuality. You're in your prime, and this is not the period of your life to be a wall-flower. Stand out.

Next, after selecting your most becoming Wingman (assuming you are not required to attend alone), set about composing your CL. How much research is necessary, or even possible, will depend on the event. Try to find out who else is going to be there. If you're not privy to the guest list, a moment of thought will probably allow you to construct much of it anyway—from the tricky relative to the work colleague the host or hostess owes an invite to. It pays to anticipate who's going to be at a party. Once, I launched into a diatribe insulting a film . . . to its set designer! I had no idea, but he took grave offense, and the dinner was a disaster. After an understandable NFI period, the hostess concerned began to include me on her invite list again, though she now always calls to **FYI** me who's on the guest list.

If you suspect conversation could get sticky, bring a prop. I have a handbag with the Maltesers logo beaded on it, into which I insert real packets of Maltesers (they're delicious chocolate malted balls) that I proceed to hand out. Doling out the "lighter-than-ordinary" choc-olate always generates a lot of excitement, except for my Wingman, who has to carry my wallet and keys because this modus operandi doesn't leave any room for inedible items.

• THE DRINKS PARTY •

Although each host thinks their event is unique, there are some standard occasions that require their own SG brand of management.

The most regular affair in your SG diary is The Drinks Party. On the glamor scale, this can range from a house party at a friend's with a pile of six-packs and several trips to the liquor store, to a cocktail party where the champagne never runs out, however hard you all try. The challenges for the SG are the same whatever the venue. You need to take charge to make sure you get through the evening without serious incident, and ensure you're sober enough to get yourself home safely afterward.

Before you head out to play, eating a meal, even if it's light, is advisable. In England we have Weetabix, a cereal that's similar to Shredded Wheat, that's a useful stomach liner. On making your entrance, do a circuit of the venue, noting bathroom facilities and likely waiting periods, and then position yourself by the kitchen. If at a posh party, this means you'll be first in line for the canapés and may actually manage to line your tummy some more. Eating is not cheating, despite whatever mantra the size-zero brigade abide by. Being by the kitchen also gives you the added bonus of meeting fun people who are most likely doing the same thing you are, being experienced party goers and often single. Indeed, I met one of my boyfriends bonding over miniature Yorkshire puddings. By the same token, kitchens are always the most packed places at house parties, and their slightly brighter lighting will discourage any potential "spotty Simons" (freaks!) from thinking they can lunge at you, while you can concentrate your attentions on more agreeable specimens.

Since you're a fabulously sociable SG who knows a lot of people, you will invariably run into people who will remember your name, while you'll be at a loss to remember theirs. Brazen exclamations like "Where have you been?" or "When did we last see each other?" work well . . . until you have to introduce them to someone else.

To help spare your blushes here, gesticulate between the two, saying "Have you met?", and proceed to take an elaborate sip of your beverage. They should then take the bait and introduce themselves to each other.

Don't panic if you turn up wearing an outfit that's identical to another girl's, even if she is four sizes smaller than you. Laugh good-naturedly, and compliment her on the one thing she has done differently, such as her lipstick shade (focusing on a part of any girl's person in a flattering fashion is always a reliable bonding tool). If the sight of your attire raised her hackles, a little fawning will smooth them back down in no time.

You may also encounter people with whom you don't wish to exchange more than mere pleasantries. Always prime your Wingman to a subtle signal—gently placing your hand on your throat, for instance—that means "rescue me." Also, agree beforehand on a gesture in case you wish to be left alone with the person you are talking to, whether it be for their banter or their brown eyes. Your Wingman will be able to cope without you; you will have picked one who can.

• THE "COUPLY" DINNER PARTY •

The next obstacle course an SG has to contend with is the "Couply" Dinner Party, held by a pair of your very married or attached friends who have a kitchen cupboard containing ramekins and springform cake pans. Beware of surprise set-ups. A good tip-off is if the host refuses you a Wingman and everyone else—save for one man—is bringing a long-term partner. These friends' ministrations will be about as understated as an Ugg boot, and your proposed new beau will probably have either intolerable prejudices, or just be looking for his first post-separation fling before he goes back to his wife and small children.

Although your initial instinct may be to decline the "couply" dinner party, you may have an interesting evening (I picked up one of my gay Wingmen from one). Arrive fifteen minutes after you were asked to, so awkward children and other halves can be settled, and bring something you want to eat or drink. If your friends are the types who have everything, bring your hostess a candle from a shop that has a classy carrier bag. Don't worry about how the candle smells or what store it was actually from, as they will never light it and will probably palm it off on someone else.

Take control by implementing your CL early, bracing yourself for the inevitable SG third-degree. You already know those first queries won't be about your health, your spectacular shoes, your flattering make-up, or even your recent promotion. It will be about your love life. This is partly so the attached inquisitor can be smug, and partly so they can live vicariously through you. Make sure you go into detail about how fun your job is, along with your spontaneous vacations and naughty playtimes. By the time you're done with them, all self-satisfied smirks will have been wiped from the skeptics' faces. You are of course open to meeting people, but at the same time you're not about to settle for substandard options. Don't defend your choices. If they don't recognize you're happy with how you're living your life, leave them to discuss garden sheds and babysitters with someone who cares.

In regaling a rapt table with an amusing anecdote in your best SG superb-value-style, a Joiner may reveal themselves. Not content with causing vacation headaches to the SG, Joiners are never off-duty. These orthodox souls—often in religion as well as outlook—will either interject a comment about your dubious morals because you had the temerity to suggest you've slept with more than one person in your life, or proffer an inappropriate suggestion. "Have you thought about the Alpha course (an introduction to the Christian faith) for meeting someone? That's where I met my [smug look] other half." A girlfriend of mine, confronted with such sanctimonious behavior, countered with a memorable—and true—riposte: "No, I'm Jewish." Joiners do not have the manners, or the self-censorship button, required, to know that you don't bring religion or politics up unless you want to destroy an evening.

At the end of the meal, always help the host or hostess clear the tables. Not only is it polite, but if you sat next to a nightmare at dinner, it means you get a break from the smallest of talk. It also allows you to surreptitiously adjust your exit strategy on your always handy cell phone if necessary, though such devices should be kept discreetly out of sight and on "silent" mode. This, along with trips to the bathroom, can provide much needed respite, allowing you to collect yourself to maintain your SG bubbliness. One note of caution: Don't make too many trips to the bathroom; then you won't have to refute rumors you're doing **dinner off the mirror**—i.e. hoovering cocaine—and/or battling bulimia.

• THE HIGH SCHOOL/COLLEGE REUNION •

Another event that brings unnecessary pressure to the SG is the high school or college reunion. The worst comes out in people at these gatherings while they seek to justify their existence over the past decade or so to their peers. If you go to one of these events, know that some attendees will decide your SG status is an Achilles heel they will zero in on to deflect their own shortcomings. That said, reunions can prove worthwhile, giving you a chance to re-connect with old friends.

Decide before you go whether you'll rise above any bad behavior and just be your usual incredible self, or whether you'll play things a little subversively. I always choose the former path, but lately the latter actually shows up at these occasions. They bring out my more mischievous side. I have not yet stooped to the level of a male friend, who hired some bling and a blonde for one college event—something that he has repented of at length because of the college's development office's incessant requests for cash. I tend to push the boundaries of appropriate dress, wearing an outfit that shows off to maximum effect a "pre-baby" body and certainly not matching the calorie consumption of a pot-bellied partner.

There are always people who take these events far too seriously, or are under the misapprehension they are actually having fun, because the last time they went out properly was the school disco in 1991. You may well look at your watch, thinking it's time to leave when only ten minutes have elapsed. However, go on to revel in seeing firsthand how happy you are to be above the rat race that so many of your contemporaries think is so important, but is actually so destructive to their well-being. You can then go on to enjoy some time with your own friends, who actually have a life.

• THE ENGAGEMENT PARTY •

Even if you are not finding another's impending matrimony bittersweet, the very nature of being an SG will cause some people to look at you at events like engagement parties with a mix of pity and superiority. As though to prolong this patronizing strike, and in direct proportion to the shrinking length of time that modern day matrimonial vows last, happy couples increasingly feel the need to stretch out their impending nuptials. If you are really unlucky, those involved will hold endless pre- and post-wedding affairs on top of the big day itself. You may find you have no choice but to turn up to them all, with no rescuing from Bunbury allowed for an occasion so significant.

You'll start off having to cope with the engagement party, where even the nicest attached people can just be irritatingly smug. Try to limit your time at it and bring a Wingman with a similar state of mind to yours. When you arrive, you will no doubt feel obliged to offer a hearty "Congratulations." If you are unsure about the union or just cannot quite bring yourself to say this, follow my GBF's tactic of expressing a supremely sincere yet utterly ambiguous "Well done." Well done for a good match? For achieving their five-year plan four years ahead of schedule? For what, exactly? It's a delightfully Machiavellian phrase, but make sure you say it before you've had one too many cocktails. You don't want to jeopardize your self-censorship faculty.

• THE BACHELORETTE PARTY •

Brides are strange souls—perfectly normal people who suddenly decide they need to have pole-dancing lessons to say goodbye to the "single" life, when they haven't been near it in years. Your status of SG will mean you'll inevitably get dragged into arrangements over the hen night; because you are someone who still goes out at night, you will probably be one of the few people Bridezilla knows who's capable of organizing it.

The one rule about bachelorette parties is: assume they're going to be dire. So manage your expectations early on. Like Christmas, they're designed for people who don't have much of a life. If the evening degenerates into a wild party, it's only because it's the first time in months the attendees have gotten out of the house. Yet at the stroke of midnight, there will invariably be an exodus as various attendees, like aged Cinderellas with shabby shoes, dash home to relieve the babysitter. Naturally, Prince Charming is not at home to look after the baby this one time because he's at the bar watching the game with his buddies.

Now indulge me a momentary lapse into cynicism, but the trend for going away for bachelorette weekends is ridiculous, especially since weddings are expensive enough to attend. You are perfectly within your rights to refuse on the basis you have to do something essential with Bunbury (who has also got me out of canoeing). If, as likely, it falls to you to organize the bachelorette party, you will be expected to anticipate the bride's wishes. Her attitude will become a cross between a relative and a diva, and instead of helpfully spelling out for you what she honestly wants, she will think it more tactful to hint. This is a nightmare, because whatever you do, you will get things wrong. One bride-to-be I know was very clear she did not want to have a fake veil or any such paraphernalia at her party, but was then devastated she did not have a prop to distinguish her from everyone else. Make it very clear at the beginning that the bridal brat has to be transparent in her briefing and must not expect you to be a mind-reader.

• THE WEDDING •

There are two distinct schools of thought about being a member of a bridal party, and you will probably already have entrenched views either way. For some SGs, if the bride is lovely, then being primped and preened and wearing a tailor-made frock will be a joyful experience. Others, myself included, firmly believe that being a "big" bridesmaid (as in aged in double figures) is nothing short of hideous humiliation. This is compounded by the attitudes of your family and even your friends, who think that because you are single, you must be lonely and therefore will want to be in the wedding party to keep busy. The bride, who is unlikely to want you looking better than her, will dress you in a less than flattering color, like bronze. And what assortment of 20- and 30-something women have figures that all look good in the same style of dress anyway?

If you want to be a bridesmaid, think long and hard about whether the bride is liable to morph into Bridezilla. You'll have to deal with her tantrums, along with those of mini members of the bridal party attired in absurd outfits the same shade as yours, warring mother-in-laws, drunken ushers—the list goes on and on. If your idea of an ideal wedding ceremony is to hide in the back pew with your PBs and giggle, before having the freedom to flit about the reception as you please with no mother-of-the-bride attending responsibilities, it can be a perfectly sensible decision to turn a bridesmaid-ship down to give yourself a chance of delighting in the wedding breakfast. Your enthusiastic expression at the nuptials might even be genuine—for the first hour of the eight-hour marathon. If you are fortunate, you will have known the person asking you to parade in taffeta for years and therefore be able to lay the groundwork for refusing volumi-nous-dress-wearing duties early, even before she has met "the one."

When a university friend got married, she was not at all offended when I refused to be her bridesmaid. I had spent almost ten years banging on about how big bridesmaids are a bad idea. It is not so easy if a new bride marrying into your family has asked you for politeness' sake. If this is the case, gently explain that being a big bridesmaid is just not "you" and kindly suggest a person whose age matches your shoe size, who would love the chance to wear a frilly dress. You could also offer to do a reading, or some other job that involves next to no work. If she complains, fake a minor breakdown bemoaning your singledom. Once you have sent her off home to her dull other half and pre-wedding diet, totter off to have a calorific cocktail with your S&MBF.

As an SG, you want to try and elicit maximum brownie points from the happy couple before the wedding to increase your chances of a good seating arrangement at the meal after. Buy them a present from their wedding list. They really don't want you to buy them something "unique." They want enough people to contribute so they have a dinner service. Also, make sure you buy your gift early so you can manage to buy a half-decent present rather than bathroom fittings or, even worse, bed linen, which I have never understood why brides-to-be think should be aired in public.

When you have dodged as many obligations as possible, the final preparation stage is to put together your "killer" outfit. An ex-boyfriend's wedding, should you be invited to it, is immediate authorization for you to max out your credit card. You must look stunning, but not too sexy. You should be allowed a Wingman for this event, but if not, and you think it may be too hard on you emotionally, don't go. I've been to an ex-boyfriend's wedding, and it was wonderful closure. I made my peace with him and my past while having a ball with several PBs. Another SG ex of his, who sat in the pew in front of me, found it harder and was in tears. Unless you were jilted by Prince William, such histrionics really aren't called for, although it is always easier to move on if you are wearing beautiful footwear.

If at all possible, try to deduce who will be attending before you go. This will also assist you in adjusting your expectations for the event. If you know your dear deaf Uncle David is coming and you are the only person he ever has anything to say to, even if it is only ever "What?", you won't feel put out when you're seated next to him. Your Wingman, thanks to a limited guest list, may not be able to accompany you; however, that does not mean you have to brave the event alone. Ask Bridezilla who else already on her guest list is in the same boat and go with them. As an SG, it's extremely useful to have a wedding partner, if only to cut the significant costs that these events entail, from sharing travel expenses, to a room at the dubious local hotel listed on the carefully worded "fact sheet" you were sent and then lost with the invite. However, set the ground rules with a traveling companion up front. A friend of mine split motel costs with a girl she hardly knew, who then scandalously brought back the groom's (divorced) dad to their room, leaving my pal without a bed for the night. If possible, I will always pre-order a car home if it is within a thirty-mile radius of my door. It costs the same as a B&B/hotel, and I will wake up in my own bed and still have some weekend time left to play with. If instead I want to after-party, there is typically someone crazy enough to offer their hotel room (and room service) for abuse, and the taxi can be put off until I am done there.

Try to act solemnly during the service itself, even if it proves unintentionally hilarious. Also find out beforehand how long the ceremony will be; I've been at ones ranging in length from ten minutes to two hours, the latter being for a "happy-clappy" wedding. Out came the synthesisers, drums, and microphones, and so did our laughter at the back of the church.

At the reception, the imbibe-alcohol-early mantra is a great tactic. You'll be anaesthetized to people at your table asking why you're an SG, and you also get the choice booze, since nothing but the un-"comped" dregs will be left by the end of the night. Also, remember to sober up during the meal. I've witnessed SGs lose control of their bodily functions at weddings, and it's never a good look. And if you're flying solo while blotto, not only how you'll get home safely will be in question, but you'll no doubt attract a number of "poor her" whisperings that will make their way to you when you've sobered up.

If you can, check the table plan early at the reception to establish your whereabouts. That way, you don't exhaust your conversation with anyone at your table before you get there. You may be temped to switch the name cards on the table to improve your draw. This is exceptionally bad form; Bridezilla will have spent months on the seating plan and the substitution will be noticed. I spied an SG relation of mine doing it once. I changed it back when she was distracted. As a result, she didn't tread on the bride's toes and had a surprisingly good time, much more so than if she had sat next to the safe bet she selected.

Your CL should keep all discussion frothy. This is not the moment to launch into deep and meaningful discussions of any description. There will be a certain quota of attendees who will focus on your alleged need to catch the bridal bouquet. Before they launch into the topic, divert them with talk of the beautiful flower arrangements. Early on in the proceedings, find a non-controversial detail—the bride's dress buttons, the sermon, the mother-of-the-bride's splendid hat—and wax lyrical about these throughout the day. You can even carry this on into the "thank you" letter, which you must send promptly to whoever mortgaged themselves to the eyeballs to pay for the lukewarm champagne and rubbery salmon.

There will probably be moments at a wedding when you will feel very "single," perhaps wistful, especially if it's a younger sibling who is tying the knot. Keep it in perspective. Focus on the Groundhog Day elements of the occasion (the conversation, the bickering relatives, the tasteless food) and this will hopefully allow you an air of amused detachment for most of the proceedings. If you truly need to act like an Eeyore, remind yourself about modern-day divorce rates.

The one good thing about a wedding is that it should be a one-off. For second weddings, using your Bunbury is allowed and you can turn down the invites. Although there are times of the year where there's a wedding glut, at least they aren't annual affairs. This isn't the case with New Year's Eve, though—an overpriced, depressing waste of time that seems to come around quicker with each passing year.

• NEW YEAR'S EVE •

January's the most depressing month of the year, and I won't accept any arguments to the contrary. The weather's foul, and no one has any money because they were paid early in December and blew it all over Christmas. Thus, there are two routes the SG can take. Either be aggressively organized and do something you were planning to do anyway—take a day trip, have a house-warming party, fork out a month's salary at a fancy restaurant—or leave New Year's to the very last minute and go with the flow.

Dismiss out of hand the pressure to find someone for a midnight kiss. Just think; by vanquishing this tradition, you are probably less likely to get ill, since there're a lot of germs floating around at that time of year. Invariably the best New Year's Eves are when you almost forget to "celebrate" midnight because you were enjoying yourself too much. My favorite New Year's Eve was planned on the day itself, when two Genuine Girlfriends came to my place for a sleepover. We drank champagne, ate yummy nibbles, and watched trashy teen movies. We were too busy ogling Keanu Reeves to switch the television over to watch Big Ben strike midnight. We woke up the next day after an early night hangover-free, with wallets intact.

• BIRTHDAY SG •

You've probably realized by now that your birthday does not belong to you; it belongs to other people. As an SG, you'll find friends, relations, and your local bartender all want a piece of you; because of this, everything will require more attention than you have time for, from guest list to venue to budget. It can be a painstaking process to get right; however, resist the urge to go Big Duvet in an attempt to pretend your birthday isn't happening. Your circle wants to celebrate *you,* and the venue or number of participants really shouldn't matter. Only a scheduled operation has gotten me out of having to plan something, so if you don't want to resort to hospitalizing yourself, I suggest going for a low-key night at that local bar. Make sure your Genuine Girlfriends are coming, tell everyone where you will be, and expect nothing. You will not be disappointed by flakes and may even end up having the time of your life when hundreds of people descend and you dance until dawn.

• FABULOUS FOOTLOOSE SG •

I am not for one minute advocating in this chapter (or anywhere else in this book) that you should plan your life so much you have no room for spontaneity. That's what being single should be all about. There's nothing like a spur of the moment event you can attend without having to notify anyone. Bunbury, escape routes, and CLs are simply ways of trying to ensure you have a good time. Your cell phone exists so you can always be in touch with friends in other locations who can advise you to turn up or stay away, because their party is either getting started or ending. "Stay in Radio Contact" is my mantra, and I regularly send spies somewhere first. If the event is any good, they text me. Nine times out of ten, I slap some lip gloss on and head out to join them. It's better to miss sleep than miss out, an attitude that would make my grandmother proud, although I'm sure she would like me to learn how to use my oven too.

The more you are out, the more you *will* be out. The preparation you do, from the CL to the fun Wingman you bring, will lead to people wanting to be around you. You'll see a domino effect in invites. On some nights you may even find yourself double or even triple parking social engagements, flitting like the social butterfly you are from occasion to occasion. You must take to heart these nights, especially when you find yourself NFI'd to an event you wanted to attend.

• NFI •

Being NFI'd is not necessarily something you should obsess over, but it is worth briefly contemplating why you were. Put yourself in the host's or hostess's shoes; there is probably a myriad of acceptable reasons. There may be a guest there you don't get along with, or the numbers are particularly tight, or it could simply be that they just forgot to invite you. Kicking up a fuss will only get you NFI'd even more, so don't make it an issue unless it's in a light-hearted and obviously teasing manner that leaves no room for misinterpretation.

If there is absolutely no good reason why they should not squeeze a fabulous SG like you in, there are other means of getting your way. Use the tactics sparingly; if you irritate anyone in the process, you'll soon enough find yourself justifiably NFI'd in the future. One SG I know who possesses a touch of the social mountaineer about her was NFI'd to a particularly high-powered dinner party. To attain an invite, she called up the hostess and invited her for dinner *à deux* at a restaurant on the same night (something the mountaineer could easily get out of going to, unlike pre-booked theater tickets), knowing full well the hostess would say that she could not attend because she had a dinner, which out of politeness the mountaineer would be invited to join instead. This principle works for most events, from bar to ball.

Then there's the "ex"-factor. The host could be better friends with him and feel that your being in the same room will be awkward. The last thing you want is for such a creature to seriously impact your social life, so take a deep breath and come to terms with both his existence and his behaviour (then and now). Even if it drives you crazy, always maintain a dignified composure in his presence. You may be crying inside, but everyone in your vicinity can see that you're fine and you're not going to ruin the vibe of an evening by turning on the waterworks.

Two members of my circle of friends went out with each other for years, until the man broke things off because of "work pressures." Of course, he moved on to another woman within two weeks, in a particularly male manner. My SG friend was just leaving a nightclub at 3 a.m. when he pushed past her to bundle another woman into a Cabbage, loudly announcing his address. She went home and cried for twenty-four hours. Then she had to make the decision. She still wanted to see their mutual friends, and not all of them would sacrifice him for her. She acted like a grownup, made sure she was seen out there having fun even if she was around him and his new girlfriend, only breaking down in private on her Genuine Girlfriends' shoulders. The new woman in his life quickly revealed herself as a prize b★tch. His friends loathed her, and she got dumped. He now quizzes the SG about any of her love prospects, which are always far superior to his own. This has a happy ending—they're better friends than before they dated. He now buys her drinks when they are out playing, instead of making her designated driver.

• GRACIOUS GRATITUDE •

Always send a "thank you" note, or perhaps even a present, to any event host or hostess. You could even stock up a "present drawer" full of useless gifts you have received that you can palm off on others. Keep track of this, though. I was once given a box of chocolates from a friend as a thank you, which I had given to her a year before. The shop assistant had accidentally put a marker pen against the label, and the chocolates were past their use-by date, so I could tell it was the same box. Smirnoff the cat enjoyed munching them, although they did make him even more schizophrenic than usual.

With the help of these small steps, events should prove to be enjoyable rather than endurance tests. And while you're out living and loving life, you will inevitably come across a new Distraction when you least expect it. When bosses, parents, friends, and roommates are being successfully managed, you are happy, and that turns the male species into a giddy moth attracted to your contentedly flickering flame. In your best SG style, you must be prepared. Indeed, so much preparation is required that I needed two chapters to tell you how.

EVENT MANAGEMENT

Survival Tips

- Select the right Wingman for the right occasion—no Social Hand Grenades for you.
- Always have a pre-booked exit strategy.
- Get to grips with your body beautiful. You can let your individuality shine through and still look right for the event.
- Remember Bunbury and stay in permanent Radio Contact, so you can "Pull the Ripcord" as needed.

CHAPTER 7

Distraction Management Part 1 Groundwork

WE ARE ALL animals. We all have needs. Our friends require entertainment, and your dating games will fulfill this obligation. Good sex comes when you are content with the good life you've created for yourself. There is nothing wrong with having a Distraction or Object, as long as they make you smile. There is a danger, of course, that these Objects make you feel anything but content, and that's when they need to be ditched.

This chapter will help you identify your target and show you how to lay the groundwork for a romance. Your primary tool in this process is telecommunications (cell, computer, etc.). These may be the bane of the modern day SG's life; however, mastering their use is the name of the game. And it is a game; much in the same way a sports team manager prepares players before the game, so should you.

• SELECTION •

There is an actual mathematical formula for the socially acceptable age range for your Distraction. If he's an older man, double your age, then subtract seven years. For a younger man, halve your age and add seven years. So if you're 28, you are allowed to date someone up to 49 years old, or down to 21 years old. There are obviously other factors, from bedroom compatibility to breeding agendas, but if you are pushing either edge of the formula, you need to dismiss the Distraction directly. This won't stop some men from getting very strange ideas. A man a year younger than my father, and considerably over my maximum dating age, once lunged at me. I suspect I will remain in shock until my dying day. By the same token, my SG contemporaries have had moves made on them by males under the age of 18, when they were at least ten years older than the boys were. Bless the little jailbaits' cotton socks.

When you're out playing with someone, be sure he can measure up to both his expectations of himself and yours. It's not about social class or job, but rather his attitude. A corporate financier girlfriend of mine has had her most successful relationship in recent memory with an impoverished waiter/actor she met at a gig. They work similar hours, and he has the confidence to give as good as he gets. She tried to date an accountant who made the same salary as she did, but he was a nine-to-fiver and got needy when she was still in the office at 11 p.m.

Be honest with yourself about the type of boy who you will play the best—and fairest—possible game with. I once dated an extremely handsome and successful man, a real alpha male who could have any model of perfection at his beck and call. It was doomed from the start because I felt he was out of my league. I was too hung up about my cellulite around him to be happy, and he spent too much time and cash grooming himself for my taste. He subsequently went on to have a long-term relationship with a glamorous thespian, while I mis-judged things and went for his complete opposite, a man of dubious attractiveness who formed his sentences *slowwwwly* and was incapable of banter. You need someone you can frolic with on an equal footing.

Emotions, though, are hard to account for. Who is to say that the silent, smoldering sort in the corner of the club is not your knight-in-slightly-tarnished-armor? However, if you do decide to play with fire and go for a legendary Lothario, don't tie yourself in knots trying to make what can only be a fling last forever (and for the record, for a petit liaison nothing beats the enthusiasm of a younger man). I have a text relationship with a Distraction who actually adorned my wall in seductive repose on posters I tore from *Seventeen* as a uni-browed, overweight teenager. True to the cliché about celebrities, he's shorter in real life than on the screen, but still had an unmistakable magnetism on the night we met. Thankfully, it was in a very dimly lit bar, as I was having a serious "skin shocker," and he wouldn't have given me a second glance in daylight. If you're going to flirt with a Jack Nicholson type, you need to have a realistic attitude. Trying to tame Mr. Alpha ++ would have been pointless, but the fun was in the flirtation. His first text will forever remain the most exciting of my life, and I have saved it on three phones.

Beyond attempting to master the Alpha males, for karma's sake don't knowingly pursue the attached variety. Not only will some girl nick your other half if you make a habit of stealing other peoples' boys, but if the Object can deceive a fellow female, you will never know for sure that he won't inevitably betray you too. Anyway, it's unlikely he will ever abandon the other woman when he is munching his apple pie and "kissing" it as well. It can be tempting—my perfect man happens to be very married—but I will absolutely never touch him. I am a child of divorce and am not going to be a cause of it. If a man wants to be with you, he will move mountains to do so.

All prospective Distractions should be given facetious nicknames, such as "Trevor" or "Wayne," for discussing them with your friends. This will help you keep your perspective and stop boys from undermining your sense of self-confidence, which they have the ability to do all too well. A "Nigel" was awful to me, but I gained smug satisfaction every time I used his nickname with my girlfriends. Giving him a moniker he'd have loathed reduced his importance to that of a legless flea and quickened my healing process. If the Distractions are actually called such names, seriously reconsider dating them at all. It may not be their fault, but their parents chose these awful appellations and they will have moulded them in some unfortunate way. Alternatively, you can christen your Objects according to strange habits. "Woof Boy" thought it was endearing to inexplicably text me the word "woof." Did he think I looked like a canine from certain angles? He only found women attractive if they were in the size zero zone of 110 pounds or less, which I happened to weigh at the time because I was seriously ill with a thyroid problem. He was also extremely patronizing, which assuaged any guilt I felt about labeling him in such a manner. The added advantage of these types of nicknames is that they help your friends remember which of your suitors you are referring to. One girlfriend has "Ping Pong Boy," someone who takes part in the sport at organized competition level and whose conversation is as tedious as his chosen recreational pursuit. If she brings him up by his real name I don't know whom she's talking about. When the specimens are really dreadful, we don't even bother thinking up new nicknames, thus "Woof Boy II" and "Woof Boy in Training" were born.

At this pre-"kissing" stage, when you are just collecting nominations, it is absolutely acceptable to have more than one interest. You can group them into the heavyweight challengers, the middleweight matches, and lightweight pushovers. If you have more than one prospective Distraction, any rejection on their part becomes amusing, and you play a much better, cooler game with the others. Because you are juggling so many Objects, you are less likely to stalk any of them. If any of this feels tawdry to you, remember you can almost guarantee you're not the only girl on the Distraction's radar. All you're doing is leveling the playing field.

• GAME PLAN •

You are attending events with all the right SG tools: CLs, business cards, phone at the ready, and a Wingman in tow who will disappear at a signal's notice. You are thus by default putting yourself in harm's way to meet a potential Distraction and exchange details. You're almost there.

It may sound obvious, but men are not mind readers. If you identify a possible Object at a gathering, make yourself known to him. This simple fact has been known to elude one or two SGs of my acquaintance, including a SG friend who always bemoans the fact she's single, yet when she finds a man she likes will utterly ignore him. SGs, there is a difference between shyness and shooting yourself in the foot. Locate a mutual friend to make the introduction. You don't need to make your interest that obvious. Just say to the introducer, "I'm sure I've seen that man over there somewhere before at a work thing . . . what's his name again?", and they will no doubt take you over to this month's potential Distraction. Alternatively, catch his eye for a moment too long, and if he does not come to you, brush past him later while talking loudly to your Wingman about an inane subject he can easily interject on. For instance, "I'm hungry" (good double entendre potential), "Crowded in here tonight," "No, you cannot possibly equate Matt Damon's performance as Bourne to Daniel Craig's as Bond," etc. (Obviously if you want him to run away, say something along the lines of "Are you Team Edward or Team Jacob?") Once initial contact is made, ask him why he's there, what he does for a living, and look at his wedding ring finger. It's not rocket science. If all is flowing nicely, perhaps mention a film you wish to see or a new bar you would like to sample. Allow him a way in.

If digits are still not looking close to being exchanged, steer the talk round to social networking sites (Facebook, Twitter, etc.) to see if he has a page, and say you should both connect/follow/whatever is the latest term *du jour*. All these sites may be a nightmare on many levels, but at this early stage, they can help as much as they later on could hinder. Alternatively you can mention an amusing e-mail forward he just has to see, and then give him your card. A man needs some encouragement, but if there is a smidgen of interest on his part, he will take the bait, and your number (or if he's really shy/pathetic/lazy, your surname so that he can "friend request" you on Facebook). If he is proving hard to hook, move on—you spend a lot of time in the sea and know there are many fish in it.

Once you have exchanged some sort of contact mechanism, you move on to the trickiest part of groundwork-laying: getting the targeted Distraction to agree to play where you want him, and in a style that will suit your game. In today's world, there is only one way to do this—telecommunications.

The Brontë sisters had it easy. Courtship etiquette in the nineteenth century had plain, established rules, and by and large they were adhered to. Perhaps you had a little too much wine with your six-course feast and, when the men retired, you confided to your fellow lady guests and a wise old aunt (who you knew would manipulate the situation into marriage) about your feelings for your chosen one. You then floated up to bed. The worst case scenario was that after de-corseting yourself, you felt sufficiently released from etiquette's constricted bounds to write a late-night love letter. However, on awaking the following morning you realized how foolish revealing your hand in such an undignified manner would have been and you burned it.

Throughout previous millennia, there were natural safety mechanisms in place to prevent both the sexes from acting too impetuously. If the man in question had penned a rather too honest missive after a slight overindulgence with some port, he too would have had the chance to censor himself the next day. As a result, the apple of his eye would never have awoken next to him the following morning having done something she shouldn't have. He in turn wouldn't have run a mile in the opposite direction, with his thirst for that wench now quenched. From the female perspective, a woman was less likely to make the mistake of fornicating with a man whose looks in daylight were not so much brooding as bad-tempered. There was an intrinsically slower rhythm to courting that made the whole business less reckless.

Modern technology means courting is now a never-ending, fast-paced battle with rejection and romancing done at a speed our ancestors never had to cope with. Even twenty years ago, it was easier. Cell phones and e-mail were just novelties. E-mail and mobiles were primitive, obscure devices few people used, let alone abused. Not so now. Today, you go out, imbibe far too much alcohol, invariably on an empty stomach because you worked late. You decide with a clarity only cocktails can bring to make a booty text or phone call. Perhaps because you have online access at home when you totter back from an evening out, or save yourself a step with a smart phone, you write a poorly spelled and grammatically challenged e-mail of an epic length to the Object of your affection. Rarely does such communication result in a fortuitous conclusion. The nightmare—often predictable—outcome is that the Object does not respond to your proposal. Even worse is that he subsequently tells, indeed forwards, this epistle to all his friends. Of course, if he'd sent you a similarly sloppy communiqué, you wouldn't hesitate to reveal the contents to your friends, would you?

Best case scenario (to your alcohol-addled mind) is that he immediately answers your entreaty, or indeed makes the text or calls himself, and you invite him round to your place. The next morning, you wake with a sore head and both un-boy-proofed skin and apartment, wondering whether you were the first person on his list. One impish Italian man of my acquaintance regularly texts me "Ciao Bella" at 3 a.m. Fortunately I've never taken him up on his offers; invariably when I compare notes with mutual female friends the next day, it becomes apparent that they were contacted too. We SGs have deduced there are distinct patterns to his overtures, and believe he must have set up group distribution lists, which he contacts depending on his mood: "Blonde," "Brunette," and "European."

Used correctly, cell phones and computers are marvellous at reeling in your prey. However, it's far too easy to sabotage even the most promising fledgling relationship by screwing up texts and e-mails. Computers and cell phones should either come with warning labels attached that say "this equipment could ruin your life," or should have built-in, time sensitive safeguards. E-mails to certain people are unable to go out for twenty-four hours, and are then sent to a number of friends to veto before finally being sent. Texts and calls should operate on the same basis.

But they do not. And until they do, we have to deal with the all-out warfare that defines courting in the twenty-first century. I write these words of wisdom and warning with the bitter experience of someone who has seriously mismanaged all these tools in the past.

• THE COMPUTER •

For me, the rot set in—in more ways than one—in college. I got into the habit of checking my e-mail on my way to/from the college bar, even interrupting my "alcopops" for a quick login during the evening. Consequently, while I was a sprite and supple student, there began the era of the heart-stopping, hung-over checking of my "sent mail" folder the following day. However, e-mail does have its uses. It was during this unfortunate period that I discovered a despicable yet essential tool in the modern courter's repertoire: the funny or useful forward e-mail, also known as "the BCC."

 ### *The BCC*

The Blind Carbon Copy (BCC) is an essential tool almost every single person with a computer knows about, and if they do not, they should. They are liable to have been manipulated by someone at some point and been ignorant of it. A BCC is an email where those who receive it do not know who else it has also been sent to. Every single friend I have has been guilty of using the BCC at some point. Indeed, the BCC is no longer just a way of copying undisclosed recipients in on an e-mail, but has come to be a reason for sending an e-mail in itself.

The BCC normally takes the form of a funny "forward" or an announcement of some essential information, such as a change of e-mail address. It gives someone an excuse to get in touch with another indirectly, and hence saves embarrassment if they do not respond. Indeed my GBF has on occasion gotten a new e-mail address just to be able to BCC a special someone who's been on his mind. Unlike with a direct e-mail or a text or call, there is less loss of face as it is socially acceptable not to reply to a BCC. Ostensibly it is all about preventing some joker from hitting "reply all" and cluttering up everyone's e-mails with boring banter, or some swindler exploiting personal e-mail accounts for their own ends.

By sending a BCC, you are reminding the other party of your existence and:

a. You want to let them know it's OK they did not text you back (or, heaven forbid, call)

b. You want them to text/call

c. You are saying "let bygones be bygones"

d. All of the above

Confused? You should be. The BCC is all about mixed messages, or it could be about sending no subliminal message at all, which is why it is so useful. For a girl trying to subtly encourage a boy to ask her out without being too obvious or off-putting, it's a far more useful device than a cell phone. A BCC is a modern-day cupid's arrow. Men like to chase, to feel in control. They can do both if you have sent them a BCC; you have just let them know that you are amenable to an approach. On several occasions, including with Mr. Alpha ++, I have actually gone to the trouble of getting Objects to text me their e-mail address if I only have their number. I make up an excuse about an e-mail I need to send them, just so I have this extra weapon at my disposal.

At this point, it's important to note a number of caveats about the tactic. First, quadruple check you've put the Object (or Objects—it can be fun to send the e-mail to all men you have crushes on and see who responds) on the BCC line. My GBF once attempted to send a BCC to only the boys he wanted to sleep—or everyone knew he already had slept—with. Unfortunately, he put their addresses on the CC line by mistake. It was an utter disaster. The GBF never "kissed" any of them again and couldn't show his face in gay-world for at least a week for the humiliation.

If you know your Object's friends, include them on the BCC. You then ensure the e-mail will not be identified as too contrived, especially if your Object mentions you've e-mailed him about something general, such as a "save-the-date" for your forthcoming S&M party. You may want to whip him into shape on your own, but it will be a little subtler if others are invited too. Remember, the BCC is about sparing your blushes. You are merely sending out an e-mail to many friends, and on no account is it a mantrap, oh no.

Selecting the actual content of the forward is crucial. Send something amusing or useful, or information that makes you look busy/popular/important. The prepared modern girl has a "funny" e-mail folder where she stockpiles forwards specifically for moments like this, but remember to double check that you haven't sent it out to them before. Also remove the header from the previous sender. The illusion will be ruined if you are forwarding an e-mail dredged up from March of last year.

You can also put a standard "signature" on your forward as well, so they have all your details. I have gone on a number of dates after men have put the numbers I listed "accidentally" at the end of my e-mails to good use.

The time of day you send the missive is key. Lunchtime is a good time for a BCC, since it's a perfectly natural time to remember your friends. Before 10 a.m. is too premeditated and is liable to be ignored by the contact, as he will not have yet had enough coffee to apply himself to anything other than work. Never send a BCC after 7 p.m. You should be out playing, doing something (or someone) better then sending ridiculous e-mails to males. Remember that the BCC is the bait, and you need to keep up appearances.

Of course, you can go through all the steps above and still run the risk he doesn't reply. However, you'll have minimized your humiliation. If he fails to respond, do not slit your wrists—in the short term soothe your ego with the explanation he was clearly busy. Longer term, find a friend prepared to plump your feathers and get real. If he really is enamoured with you, he will always reply, and several increasingly flirty (non BCC'd, of course) e-mails later, you'll have hooked him.

The Direct E-mail

If you must directly e-mail (and when chasing a man who really has not wanted me I have resorted to this tactic), try to make it short and have it contain a pertinent question that only he can give a suitable reply to. For example: something pertaining to his area of work expertise, or suggestions on what to buy a very good mutual friend for their birthday. One girlfriend of mine actually drafts e-mails to her Objects, then sends them on to me to edit. We had to introduce this rule after she e-mailed an amour before their second date asking whether it was time their parents met. Her stalker status was not only assured, she was one step away from a restraining order. Now when she e-mails, she BCC's me so that I am kept abreast of the situation.

The question mark is a key indicator to where the parties stand when directly e-mailing. The reason? It's rude not to reply to an e-mail with a question mark in it. The keener party, the sender, knows this, and will therefore use one. If the respondent is interested, they will themselves insert a question into their reply. If they don't reply, move on. Either they are useless at e-mailing and will do something constructive like call you later, or they just do not want to "kiss" you.

A word of warning on direct e-mailing: One notorious playboy cautions to never send an e-mail with the subject heading "Hey." He literally shivered as he motioned with his fingers hitting "delete" on his keyboard. "Hey" indicates that the contents of the e-mail will be needling, invariably trying to elicit a date or girlfriend status from him, and immediately puts him on the defensive.

As with the BCC, pick your moment when sending the direct e-mail out. If you know he is going to be hung-over, try for 11.30 a.m. He will be counting down the minutes to sandwich-buying time and craving sympathy for his massive headache.

He-mail Banter

So, you have BCC'd or directly e-mailed him, and he has replied. If he has BCC'd or directly e-mailed first, even better, but we all know modern boys are lazy and often need a smidgen of encouragement. A reply within minutes is a very good sign, as this is an invitation to indulge in "He-mail" banter; a rapid succession of funny, flirty e-mails that may just get you the date you are trying to engineer.

There is no substitute for experience here. Some advocate playing hard-to-get and waiting for a few hours before replying. Whatever the case, it's important to attend to all the minor details of how your e-mail looks and reads. Develop a regular sign-off in e-mails. Mine used to be "Lots of love" followed by three kisses. This scared off one suitor, who did not realize it was standard. I now use my initial, 'I', followed by one little kiss. If I put just kisses, and lots of them, this is someone I like. If I am worried about encouraging someone I am not into, I lose the kisses completely. Take the tone of your sign-off from him. If he is leaning on the 'x' button and you really like him, you can too, but always make sure you send slightly fewer kisses. Never send more. If you want to keep the caveman interested, he needs to believe he is chasing you.

Also, remember e-mails can be recorded and forwarded. Just ask Claire Swire, a poor girl who e-mailed her Object a graphic description of how much she had enjoyed an intimate interlude with him, and it went worldwide like wildfire. E-mail sex can be unbelievably hot, but you are then forever living in fear.

Some computer systems and Web sites have Instant Messenger (IM), where you can see whether targets are online and instantly connect by popping up a message on their screen. IM is a dreadful invention unless you are in a relationship and having IM sex. Otherwise, it has nothing to commend it whatsoever. You're inevitably

IM'ed when you, the multi-tasker, are busy at work, so imagine how a boy with a one-track mind will feel if he is actually in the middle of something vital. Never, ever, ever, IM a boy first.

IM also creates awkward situations. One lovely boy who refused to believe I didn't share his ambition to move from London to a place where you cultivate cabbages instead of hailing them, declared his undying love in the middle of an IM conversation he began. I didn't want to be disturbed anyway, as I was getting all taxed by my tax return, but he could see I was logged into the network. Talk about putting me on the spot! After a panic-stricken online silence, I opted for the "laugh it off" option and treated the declaration as a joke. I almost saved face for everyone involved, until a member of his IT department who had been monitoring the exchange forwarded the transcript around his company. Such "Big Brotherly" love.

Bouncing Unwanted Males

We all need the "ego boost" boys; they help negate the ego-battering variety. Some males, though, need to get the message that you are simply not interested. Attempt not to resort to rudeness unless you really have to. Remember how you would feel if you were in their position and treat them as you would be treated.

The rules to get rid of such a boy are simple. Just flip the tips above. Never send him a BCC; never respond if he e-mails you one. And if he sends you an e-mail with a question, although it is only polite to get back to him, leave your response for a few days and do not include a question of your own. If he instant messages you, say that you are sorry but you are manic and need to go, then close the IM window.

Eventually he will get the message. Otherwise, call the courts.

The Internet

Forget being a research tool for scientists: The Internet was clearly invented to investigate potential conquests, and if you are lucky, your Object will have some cyberspace listings. The crafty courter will use tools such as Google, Instagram, and Facebook. These sites can be exceptionally helpful, not only for asking the right questions, but pitching your level of interest in, for instance, the rise of eco-friendly big business. They can also reveal skeletons in your prospective Distraction's closet, thus helping you decide whether he's worth your valuable SG time.

Once, out on the prowl with my GBF, we met a beautiful boy, the only one we have ever competed for. We both thrust out our chests, pushed our shoulders back, and launched ourselves on him, dribbling so much that pools of saliva formed at our feet. I won the battle, and the man in question spent four weeks trying to track down my phone number (I let him leave without giving it to him, as his parents had suddenly materialized by his side). In a fit of jealousy, the GBF teased me that the gorgeous boy was years younger than me and I was venturing into cradle-snatching, rather than boy toy, territory. After all, he was out with his mother! One Google search and some labored mental arithmetic later confirmed he was, in fact, thirteen months older, and I was absolutely allowed to date him.

The Google image search can also be invaluable if you met your Object while marginally merry in a darkened room. Thanks to the explosion of Facebook and the like, many a male posts pictures, if not a blog, online. It is important to remember, however, that information gleaned from a Web search may be inaccurate. One of my male confidants shares a name with a porn star. Although my friend has been notorious for his promiscuity in the past, and videoing his nocturnal activities is not something his friends would put past him, he's not a Boogie Nights boy. If I Google myself, a pile of incorrect information, not to mention some very dubious photos, appears. Before we met, my publisher saw that I was listed as 7 years old. Were they doing a deal with a child?

It is not a good look to reveal that you have Googled your Object. Ever. Doing an Internet search on a prospect is a bit like using the BCC. Everyone knows it is there, everybody does it, but nobody admits to it. My GBF was so well-informed about one of his dates that the Distraction realized he had been Googled, suspected he was out with a stalker, and swiftly swept out of the cocktail lounge. Remember you are not supposed to know this information you've discovered. Let them tell you. Internet research can simply allow you to create a very good CL, which with luck will not be required anyway, as the pair of you will be getting on like Johnny and Baby after he fished her out of the corner.

The Internet also has more obvious options—the online love affair with someone you meet on a blog/dating, etc., site. I hold a deep suspicion of starting a relationship with someone you have not actually met. Yes, computers can be used to elicit dates, but from my experiences, described in Chapter Five, it does truly help if you have some real-life knowledge of what the other party involved looks like first. No one is going to be honest if they write a description of themselves, and any photo they select is going to be dimly lit and Photoshopped enough to imply that they are more Johnny Depp than Keith Richards.

Dating a keyboard is dubious. Meeting your online love in person? Take a Wingman, and keep your phone handy.

• THE CELL PHONE •

Freud would have needed decades to analyze the havoc this small device has caused to our society. My cell is my contact with everyone; it is my business, family, friend, lover, and, when my Object's not in touch, my enemy. Without my phone, I feel naked, exposed, incomplete. The trauma that losing a phone incurs—the missing numbers, texts, and photos—is a nightmare not to bear thinking about.

When I get my annual cell phone upgrade, it's a massive decision over which new model will be mine. Then there is the cleansing process: Only a certain number of names and texts can transfer on my SIM card to the new phone. Which business contacts are in? Which boyfriends are out? Which texts do I leave behind? Which lovers do I finally close the book on? Changing phones causes me to reflect on my life more than any birthday does. The cell is the modern-day person's version of a journal, where sinful secrets and mundane matters are stored. Suspicious other halves no longer need sneak a peek at someone's diary. For all SGs, the cell phone is the most intimate point of contact with the Object besides being in his presence. It is where his tender texts are saved, and where his 3 a.m. calls appear in the "phone log."

The cell phone game is high roller territory, and, as such, the stakes are highly speculative. You could win it all, but there is the ever-present risk that you can lose everything, too. To minimize the threat of having to declare a love "bankrupt," start by organizing your address book. Make sure the telephone numbers of exes or current interests are not the first number in your Contacts section or stored near taxi numbers/BFs. As one male Lothario of my acquaintance says, "Everyone needs an Aardvark" (a phony first entry on their phone), otherwise an accident is inevitable. Almost everyone has a sob story that is the result of an inept listing. A girlfriend was doing very well in ignoring a man who was bad for her. She hadn't contacted him for weeks and disregarded all his attempts at communication, until one day she accidentally dropped her phone and it rang him up—her contact book was sorted alphabetically and his was the first name listed. She ended up getting back with him and had an even more traumatic break-up several months later.

When you have an Object's number safely stored, you should then allocate him his own ring and message tones. I have returned phones after discovering that they don't have these functions. Customized chimes save the endless agony of hoping it's him when your phone makes a noise, then finding that it is just something unimportant, like your credit card company flagging a large purchase from a shoe shop. Remember to switch your phone onto vibrate when you are with people who might tell him or, quite rightly, laugh.

These are all ways to make this compulsory courting tool more bearable; yet, like the computer, your cell can be manipulated to help the predator trap her prey. However, not even the masters or mistresses of the cell will get it right all the time. Even though we know we should not drink and dial, accidents can, and do, happen.

The Text Message

There are two types of people in the world. Those who almost always respond immediately to all texts (me) and those who do not (the majority of the population, apparently). You will very quickly discover which one your Object is, and you must adjust your behavior accordingly. There are some basic rules, however, when it comes to the text game:

- Try never to be last to text. The old saying "leave them wanting more" is definitely true here. If it is unavoidable, so be it, but remember this looks especially bad if you are the one who instigated the exchange.

- Do not "double text." Don't be the last to text, and then first with a new subject, unless there's a very good reason. Wanting to know how he's doing or to tell him that you miss him is not a good enough excuse. If you are ever tempted to double text, please call your friends first and consult. Then refrain.

- Kisses, as in e-mails, are a minefield. If in doubt, put a smiley face instead of a kiss. Or just leave it. If he returns with two kisses, you're in business.

- Capital letters mean SHOUTING! Lower case them unless you are joking or very cross indeed.

- Like e-mail, if you want a reply to a text, include a question mark. Otherwise recipients can ignore them. If they neglect to reply at this point, it is not disastrous, especially if they are the sort who never text back, but it's not looking good if they are normally of nimble thumb.

➤ If you know you are liable to text the Object, but also know it's crucial that you don't, brief some friends and then text them instead when you are struck by an overwhelming need to contact him. Sometimes it is just a case of keeping your fingers and phone busy to prevent a communications error. If need be, give your cell to someone else to look after until the moment has passed. Or write the Object's number down and delete it off your phone. You'll think twice about texting if you have to locate it and type it in.

On the whole, I try not to day-text Monday to Friday. There is always e-mail, which is less invasive and, at certain times, permissible during working hours. If a boy is in full professional flow, he won't take too kindly to being interrupted. If you must day-text, do not expect an immediate response, and try to leave at least ten minutes before replying if he texts you. You have far more weighty things to attend to.

After 6 p.m., answers can be immediate. It's now time for flirtatious repartee. There are some tactics for evening hours, but realize you're in a risky, winner-take-all contest, with possible humiliation lurking around the corner with every move.

There does exist the cell phone equivalent of the BCC. The "group" text is when you send out the same text to a number of contacts. Use this sparingly, perhaps if you don't have his e-mail address, or if it's over New Year, when nobody attractive should have e-mail access. Unlike the BCC, group text options are very limited. "Happy New Year" is fine; texting your birthday arrangements, again OK. I have delved as low as a "who's playing tonight?" text, but that was quite frankly embarrassing. It worked, but the abashment lasted longer than the liaison.

I am a fan of textual healing. This is a quick note to get a relationship back on track, whether it be a friendship endangered by an accidental "kiss," or an argument you need to apologize for. I always send these communications early evening or on weekends, at a time the recipient knows I must be sober, so they're not misinterpreted as some sort of veiled bed-beckoning transmission.

In helping develop a situation with an Object, an empathetic text about their hangover the day after you have seen them out on the town and know that they are going to be feeling rough can work wonders. Men like sympathy, so if they are suffering from the "man flu," aka a runny nose, a "get well soon" text will also no doubt reach appreciative thumbs.

There is also the strategy of mistakenly sending a text to someone on purpose. You and your friends know that you would never send a text in error because you have arranged your phone book listings accordingly. Your latest Object will not. You could therefore send a text making yourself look busy and in demand. For example: "So sorry, am running late, but will be there soon . . . x." If he gets back to you, apologize, for in your haste you mistakenly texted the Object rather than your friend above him in your listings. This is a regular ploy for a gay friend of mine, and it usually gets stellar results, but it's wiser, as with the group text tactic, to use this sparingly, too, since it is a bit obvious.

We now enter the high-risk zone—the booty text, the late night emergence of a message in your Object's trousers. If you are going to perform a late night booty text, try and make it relatively subtle (as subtle as a text sent after midnight can be) so as to avoid next day/week/year/lifelong humiliation. Perhaps you have seen him out or know he is going out, in which case "Hope your head doesn't hurt tomorrow x" is a relatively safe text to send. As long as he knows you didn't set your alarm to wake you at midnight to send the text especially and that you are actually out yourself. This gives him a window of opportunity to get in touch at 3 a.m. saying he wants to come round for some nocturnal activity. If not, he is just left with an aching head the following day and a sympathetic message. "I want you now big boy" doesn't work as well when he has awakened up next to another girl, feeling like death, but very pleased with himself all the same. It will merely serve to inflate his ego all the more, even if a certain part of his anatomy is a temporarily deflated force.

Finally, please try not to send pictures or videos of yourself naked. He will either lose the phone, his friends will steal it, or he will show pictures of you naked to them anyway.

Hopefully, you will soon get past the text message obstacle-course stage. If a man wants to conduct a relationship almost always by virtual means of communication and rarely sees you, then he is **All Text No Trousers,** and the little **Clit Teaser** needs to be sent on his way. Real romances require the exchange of bodily fluids.

 Calling

Unless you are in a relationship, do not call. Like barbecuing, it is one of the few jobs that remain for the male species, and it is wrong to deprive them of it. Texts are sufficient for the females. Girls have a tendency to be useless on the phone to boys anyway. According to one predatory male, females should never leave voicemails because they get flustered and humiliate themselves. It is not as if there is a need to leave one anyway. If you do call, your number will pop up under "missed calls," the modern equivalent of calling cards. If he never calls back, he is call screening. Take the hint.

Keep in mind that if a man wants you, he will find his way to you. If he fails to e-mail, text, or call, his computer and phone may be broken or stolen. He could also be in another country unable to crack the local dialing codes. However, if a man wants you and one type of communication fails, at some point in the near future he will try another. If it has proper potential, meeting should really not be that hard. Thus we turn to the next step.

The date.

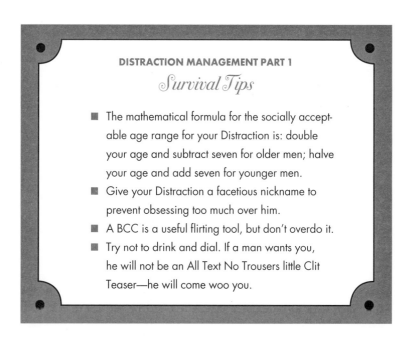

CHAPTER 8

DISTRACTION MANAGEMENT PART 1

Survival Tips

- The mathematical formula for the socially acceptable age range for your Distraction is: double your age and subtract seven for older men; halve your age and add seven for younger men.
- Give your Distraction a facetious nickname to prevent obsessing too much over him.
- A BCC is a useful flirting tool, but don't overdo it.
- Try not to drink and dial. If a man wants you, he will not be an All Text No Trousers little Clit Teaser—he will come woo you.

Distraction Management Part 2
Kissing, Etc.

*T*HE PRE-MATCH deliberations are over, and you've made your selection; now it's time to play the game. At all stages keep in mind why you are putting yourself through these sometimes exhausting encounters: entertainment—for the enjoyment your friends will obtain from the debriefing the following day, and the anecdotes that you can subsequently regale forevermore because of the rendezvous. You may also get some "kissing" out of it.

This chapter is about the physical interaction you have with your Distractions, from dates to the exchange of bodily fluids. At all times you need to keep in mind one word: fun. For if the exchanges you are having with your Object do not have a frisson of fun about them, then what is the point? These initial moments with him (or her, as I touch on bisexuality too) are supposed to be the delicious stage. If they aren't, you need to get out of the entanglement and start the selection process again as soon as possible.

• THE DATE •

 The Proposition

A proper Distraction is one that you see in person and go on a date with. Now, "date" is a loose, informal, unofficial term, covering everything from hanging out at each other's places to being swept off your Choo-clad feet (a pre-rendezvous present, naturally) and into a Venetian gondola. If any of the following occurs—you're alone with a boy you like; you shave your legs; you wear matching underwear; you boy-proof your flat; you alert friends to the meeting's occurrence—it's a date.

The definition of a date does not include everything, of course. If your Distraction has brought friends to talk to and ignores you, he isn't interested. I once turned up to what I thought would be a romantic dinner, and instead we "accidentally" bumped into two of my Object's male friends, who he insisted joined us. This heavy-handed and unsubtle method of protection lacked finesse, but then we were barely out of our teens at the time. I have subsequently come across men who execute this maneuver with admittedly slightly more style, but who carry it out nevertheless. Also, be wary of any meet-up with your Object that occurs between the hours of 10 p.m. to 3 a.m. More than one supremely desirable rake I know believes that any dalliances during these hours don't count. You absolutely count, so don't become one of them.

There may be certain proclivities that are no-goes for you, in which case make your position known early on. Men who do coke are a big turn-off for me because, apart from anything else, males who hoover can never get it up when you require them to. Within minutes of meeting a potential someone, I will therefore have relayed an amusing anecdote that states my position in no uncertain terms. It is sad but true that for most SG friends of mine, more than one relationship has stalled because the man is already in one with one too many substances.

On the flip side, there seem to be a growing number of men who are completely clean. I recently went to a singles dinner party in Hollywood where none of the men were drinking. All the girls were, albeit in moderation, but we suddenly felt like the hardest partiers on the planet (it was probably because we were in LA). Be wary of extremes. Abstinence could mean your Distraction is driving, or they're health freaks . . . or they're in recovery for addiction to something slightly more potent than a skinny moccachino. Of the four men at this particular dinner, only one was driving. The rest had "issues." Such addictions should be red-flagged and considered carefully early on. Don't dip your toe in the water if you feel the current will be too strong for you to cope with.

Once you have settled on your target, in a casual (but, let's face it, probably contrived) way, you need to meet with the Object and actually do something together. Occasionally, you may find yourself agreeing to a mercy date with a man who has pursued you so much and got mutual friends to beg on his behalf to such an extent that it becomes rude not to give him his chance. Or it could be accidental. I have assented before to a date on Instant Messenger because I was concentrating on work, rather than the cyber conversation.

A brief word of warning for those prone to not leaving their house if the daily Horrorscope texted to their phone says they are in for an inauspicious day. In the run up to the date, I know it's tempting to sneak a little look at your and his star signs in each magazine you pass in the supermarket line. These "premonitions" aren't useful for anything other than wrist-slitting. One SG I know actually went against her better judgment and followed a Horrorscope that said she was destined to fall in love with someone she met near a red door. While at a house party—the front door was red—a man asked her out and she agreed. Mutual acquaintances were agog; he was duller than dishwater. On their first date, Dishwater Man lived up to his reputation and proceeded to take our sparkling SG though about two hundred of his holiday snaps, before asking her to choose her three favorites. There was no second date, but he took months to get the message, sending a succession of e-mails with the subject heading "Hey." (I sense collective SG shuddering after the lessons learned in Chapter Seven.)

 ## The Setting

The male species still like to believe they control the variables of the date. *Let* them. Allow him to suggest a venue, but, if necessary, steer him toward a place you find acceptable.

If the date was arranged accidentally or under duress, then opt to meet in daylight and have lunch or coffee. Dinner à deux in a notoriously romantic restaurant is not what the doctor ordered (yet). If by some miracle you and your companion do get along, you can then up the location ante on subsequent meetings. For now, if you suspect that the man is the type where you'll only have enough to say for a *lunch*, keep it to that. If a waiter sees a couple for dinner, they may assume you want to linger, and slow the service accordingly. There will be no such error made before 6 p.m., and you can be in and out within an hour.

For the slightly better prospect, someone perhaps you're on the fence about, meet for drinks. If you are getting on famously, you can then go on to dinner. If not, you can go and join Bunbury. For all early dating scenarios, until you know what kind of Distraction you are dealing with, ensure the Object knows all about the unfortunate Bunbury and their unpredictable demands on your time. Through a series of texts that you've primed your friends to send at appropriate points in the evening, Bunbury can always cancel on you halfway through the rendezvous. Your Distraction can then rescue you from the sudden gap in your social schedule in knight-in-*dining*-armor fashion.

Your Distraction's behavior during the planning stage of the date will indicate a good deal about him. If he takes control, listens to your preferences, and then arranges something wonderful, having thought everything through, this is probably someone you want to spend time with. If he is indecisive and picks a venue that serves food that would not be out of place on *Fear Factor*, your evening probably won't improve. Although your initial instinct may be to cancel the encounter altogether, until you've actually spent time with him, you cannot be sure how things will pan out. A fair player should give an Object a sporting chance. My BF had a boyfriend who suggested bowling for a first date. Audience participation is not her thing; she prefers to be entertained, not to be the entertainment. She also disliked the concept of enforced shoe-ditching, meaning you cannot run away if necessary. Before my BF pulled out altogether, a PB pointed out that at least the boy was showing initiative in neither suggesting a dingy diner nor delegating the arrangements to her. The BF tactfully suggested a picnic, an activity more to her liking. Love almost blossomed with the birds and the bees, until both types of wildlife got over-amorous with their food, causing this bird and bee to find refuge in the nearest . . . diner.

If the choice of venue is left to you, don't suggest a place you regularly frequent with friends, at least in the early stages. If it all goes horribly wrong, you will never be able to return to your favorite pub/bar/restaurant. Naturally your taste is so good he will attempt to steal your stomping grounds, meaning you can't go back without fear of bumping into him. Early on in my dating career I was careless enough to do this, and after running into the man more times than I cared to, I was forced to change playgrounds.

 ### The Costume

Once the venue is selected, make sure your outfit matches accordingly. Sporting events do not require *Stella McCartney*, unless you're attending on the arm of her dad and attempting to be appointed Lady Macca the Third. The Object's attire is equally significant, though having a Distraction who spends more time and disposable income on shoe shopping than you is just distressing. A man can be too **Metrosexual.** By the same token, **Retrosexuals**, cavemen types who are inordinately proud of their scruffiness and lack of grooming habits, can be just as disagreeable. One lawyer SG friend invited an Object to a Christmas party of one of her clients, an oil firm. To make a stand for the environment, the strict veggie PC sort showed up unshaven, wearing plastic shoes and a pungent fleecy jacket that had once been mustard in color, but was now a stylish turd-like shade of brown. My friend had to ditch him on her doorstep and call up her GBF for emergency suited-and-booted Wingman support.

The Banter

Your CL will certainly contain questions pertinent to your Object, since it is useful to find out his views to ascertain whether he is worth spending any more of your time with or not. Since men like talking about themselves, this should be no hardship for him, although it may be for you. One SG I know had to endure a three-hour dinner date during which the Distraction spent the whole time talking about himself. By the end of the evening, he still did not know what my friend did for a living. To cap it all off, he picked a dome-lifting tastic pricey restaurant, and after ordering the most expensive champagne and wine on the menu, made her pay half. She was 22 and obviously didn't have the cash. Hell hath no fury—later, at a law firm's dull drinks party, she came across his boss, who asked her opinion of the man. She let rip about his Scrooge-like people skills, which proved the catalyst for him subsequently being fired.

Establish your Object's activity levels and interests early. One SG friend is having a lot of fun with a rock climber, as she too possesses a fetish for climbing the Rockies on weekends. Of course it is not compulsory for you to share every pastime; it's healthy to have separate ones, but a few common interests will help. I am quite happy for a man to be passionate about footie (what the rest of the world calls soccer). As long as he's fine with me grooming myself with my girlfriends, I'm fine with him watching men hug each other on a Saturday. Sometimes, though, similar mind-sets on certain matters are useful. If his idea of spending a Sunday is running a marathon while your preferred pastime is sex, your differing outlooks may be insurmountable.

Your CL should also be in keeping with the date's venue. If the Object is taking you somewhere that involves some specialized knowledge, call up a friend who knows a lot about that particular activity. Never pretend you are an expert, especially since men relish that role, but your friend can instruct you on good questions to ask. Online research can help, but be wary of anything that you are not directly told. A lovely man once suggested a date to the movies and left the film selection up to me. A Google check told me he was into foreign art house films, but turns out the trusty search engine was anything but. I had to wake the Distraction up halfway through the movie, he was snoring so loudly. Later, I admitted I was just trying to impress him with my "cultural" leanings (I obviously couldn't reveal the real, cyber-stalking reason), and over a bottle of wine we discovered we were both lowbrow movie buffs who prefer their flicks of the blockbuster/Bond variety.

There are some safe, general topics to oil the conversation's wheels if your research exhausts itself or proves inaccurate. Vacations are always a reliable conversation vein. Invariably people need, have just come back from, or are deciding on one. This will also help you determine whether you are remotely compatible. One potential lover didn't even bother to lunge (try to kiss) on goodbye once he realized a mini-break involving me sleeping in a tent on a glacier really wasn't an option.

The **iPod Icebreaker** is another dependable conversation ploy. Ask your date what the most embarrassing song on his iPod is. If he has a sense of humor about it, it's always a good sign, and the song he chooses will also say an awful lot about him. Mine is Boyzone's (UK's answer to N'Sync) version of my dad's "No Matter What." It's a secret boy band fetish and daddy idolization rolled in one: no wonder I'm single! If you want a snapshot of his deepest, darkest secrets, all you need to do his look at his "Most Played" playlist. If you find one too many show tunes, pass him on to your GBF immediately.

If the date goes spectacularly, you may not have to resort to your CL; however, it's always preferable to have one in reserve, as the fear factor can sideswipe any SG's chatter if there's a pair of puppy-dog brown eyes transfixed on her. Conversely, you may find yourself in the company of someone exceptionally dull, at which point the CL will make the time flow by much more quickly. If you are controling the conversation, then at least there are no excruciating silences. Just try to stifle your yawns, although perhaps do not hide your boredom too well, merely for politeness' sake. One SG girlfriend went on a date with a man who was so dull she exhausted every last topic on her CL. He took the non-stop discussion as a sign of their compatibility and spent the next year using his online blog to dedicate soppy, badly spelled poetry to her. She still lives in fear that any Object she actually wants may Google her and find the lamentable verse.

Demeanor

Your behavior will vary according to location, from life and soul at a bar (although still letting him get his word in edgeways), to quietly contemplative at an art gallery. However, there are some obvious guidelines to adhere to at all times.

Try not to get blindingly drunk. Not only do men find it unattractive, you may also do something you regret. Of course, I obviously do not speak from personal experience here, oh no . . . If you are having drinks, alternate them with water, especially if you will be moving on to wine with dinner later.

Men like to feel like men, so when you're at the movies let them hold the tickets and the popcorn. During the film you can therefore choose whether or not you put your hand in the area around his crotch, and with what regularity. You'll also ensure he's the one more likely to have popcorn stuck all over him when the credits roll.

When you're out for a meal, don't be disturbed if he refuses to talk until he has ordered. Men have one-track minds, and he might only be capable of making one decision at a time. Also avoid tricky food. If you are eating pasta, opt for penne instead of spaghetti. If you think you may want to kiss him, lay off the garlic and spring onions, unless he doesn't. Of course, if you decide you want him nowhere near you, eat as much odoriferous food as you like.

While at dinner, remember you're also there to eat. SGs who order a salad and subsequently fret over how they're sacrificing their diet will have their boy dismissing any subsequent off-menu capering with you quicker than he can say "I must go find Bunbury". In general, don't get hysterical about food in his presence. One PB stopped dating an SG because she was scared of peas and sweet corn. If some sort of outburst is inevitable, then try to make it endearing. I suffer from "food rage," intense jealousy of what anyone with me has ordered. To counteract this, I'll either have what he is having, or state early on that I may want a taste of his dish (obviously, exercise caution with that phrase). Sharing can be very sexy; indeed someone's approach to food is normally a good indicator of their approach in the bedroom. Now is the perfect time to assess the potential of those skills.

Gourmands tend to appreciate and know what they are doing between the sheets. Fast eaters are a little too swift in that department, and fussy eaters somewhat straight-laced. Another good indicator of accomplished bedroom prowess is dancing. A man who is a good dancer, taking the lead in a firm, but gentle, oh-so-sexy way, is universally acknowledged to be someone who will, well, simply shag you senseless in a superior manner.

I am always suspicious if a date eats less than me and refuses to order dessert. How can he be a real man? He must either be doing his dinner off the mirror, be bad in bed, or both. An agent I met on a business trip to LA sent me on a blind lunch date. The man was a producer of a major TV show, but it soon became clear that we were completely incompatible. Mr. Producer had been to a wrap party the night before, where he was freaked out by his over-indulgence of two vodkas. He then refused to eat anything straight off the menu, insisting everything had to be gluten/sugar/fat/fun-free. Heaven forbid if the dressing arrived any way other than on the side. If I'd wanted to witness a lunchtime temper tantrum, I would have opted for visiting one of my toddler-toting friends.

Your date is going really well if neither of you looks at your cell, but if you spend the evening replying to all the friends you arranged to text you so you look popular, give up and go find Bunbury. If he spends the night texting, likewise give up and go find Bunbury.

It is traditional for a man to pay during these early stages, but since you're a modern woman, always offer, even if you do not expect to actually fork out any money. If you've been on a few dinner dates with a man who is more financially stretched than you, it may be tactful to go to the bathroom and subtly pay en route. Or if he leaves the table, take the opportunity to pay the bill then. This ensures his dignity's intact. He can jokingly complain that you've paid while being slightly relieved that he doesn't have to face the potential indignity of his credit card being refused.

The last hurdle of the date is how to handle the goodbye. If you do not want to kiss the Distraction, you run the risk of being lunged at if you linger too long, so take control of the situation as you say farewell. Usually a quick but firm peck on the cheek before swiftly departing works. I'm trying to train an SG friend who thinks it impolite not to kiss a man if he has taken her out, that it's ruder to snog someone and disappear off the face of their earth, than to opt for a more chaste cheek peck. Additionally, if you don't live in an apartment building, you may find it helpful to invest in a security light for your front door. Not only can they scare off burglars, they may frighten away Objects you don't want to kiss. An SG friend installed one outside her door and now "forgets" to inform any date she does not want to kiss about the impending illumination. While he does the dazed "rabbit-in-the-headlights" look, she has just enough time to rush inside alone and go play with a more appealing kind of rabbit.

A man's behavior at the end of the date says so much. Some are hopeless, but others can take chivalry to a new level. One Distraction I was unsure of earned a second date because when I got into a taxi, he handed over a crisp twenty-dollar bill to the driver and told him to make sure I got home safely. It wasn't about the money; no (straight) man had ever behaved so gallantly with me before. I told my brother the tale, and he said he constantly made the same gesture. No wonder he is always attached. The birth of the modern independent woman does not mean society should suffer the death of old-fashioned manners.

Post-date

There are only two scenarios after the date. Either you want another one (or are of two minds about him enough that he is to be rewarded with a second hearing to help you reach your verdict), or you don't.

It's easier if you have decided the Distraction is not for you. Ditching is covered in more detail in the following chapter, but at this early stage, all you need to do is text him "thank you" at the end of the evening, then don't contact him again. If he phones your cell from his phone, don't answer. If he calls you from an unidentified number and you accidentally pick up, tell him he got you "at a bad time" or you are "in a meeting." Then, don't return his phone call, instead leaving it a few days before e-mailing or texting him in response to anything he has asked you. Don't ask any questions in return, and make it clear you are utterly manic for the foreseeable future. This keeps things polite but clearly disinterested. You also do not necessarily want to alienate a new friend, as his circle could be packed with other potential Objects that you would like to distract yourself with.

In the circumstance you do want another date, do not text him "thank you" at the end of the evening, since you are then prematurely playing all your cards. Wait and leave yourself the option of texting or e-mailing him "thank you" first thing the next morning. By leaving your expression of your gratitude to the following day, you create the opportunity for banter and have made it easier for him to suggest another encounter.

If you desire this particular Distraction, remember the following truth uttered by one of London's most eligible bachelors (mothers and fathers positively unlock their daughters as far as he is concerned). If a man wants to be with you, he will find you. Post-date, follow the golden rule that passive is active. Bombarding him with missives is not cool. If you want him, you must hold your nerve. Again, this comes from my (very) bitter personal experience! If he's really serious it could take him a few days to ask you out again. One SG friend recently had to wait almost a week for her Distraction to get back in touch after what she thought was a phenomenal date. It turns out it was so good that he got scared and had to decide whether he really did want a girlfriend or not. He then dropped his phone down the toilet and spent several more days trying to track down her number, heroically withstanding the consequent mocking he got from everyone he contacted, plus the mutual friends they in turn told.

Occasionally you may bypass the date stage and go directly to the "kissing" one. If you want "kissing" to be a repeat occurrence, especially if you kissed in a random non-date situation, such as a clinch in a club's corner, you are not allowed to contact him the following day. You will get nowhere. Every SG who contributed to the research for this book agrees. The day after the kiss, don't lower yourself to carrying out the chasing chore. Leave it to him.

Now, you may still have more than one Distraction in play. There are some advantages to dual or even triple dating. The less you care about a particular Object, the more aloof you are, which makes you that much more attractive to a man—they are suckers for the challenge of the chase. In New York City, for example, it's perfectly acceptable to be dating a number of men. One New Yorker SG I know actually asks a man how much he earns before she even agrees to go out with him. The Big Apple's boys are so used to this behavior that they tell her without hesitation, while in other places asking this question would be deemed the sole realm of the gold digger.

When it comes to the number of Distractions you are juggling, follow this golden rule. If you are having a problem justifying the number of men you're dating to yourself, there is a problem. If you've gotten to the exchanging bodily fluid stage with several men you're seeing, you may be getting an SG reputation you do not want.

• KISSING •

The exchange of bodily fluids with your Distractions is a delicious naughtiness that may be an outcome of any of the scenarios described above. This should be the really fun part of dating. If it is not, serious re-consideration of your involvement with the Distraction is in order.

The terms "kiss" or "**kiss and cuddle**" have become polite euphemisms to refer to anything from a slight snog (making out) to full-on sex. The actual kiss is a useful tool in helping an SG decide how far to take a Distraction physically. If he is a bad kisser and a nice person, it may be tricky. There are some men who can be taught, but if he is really awful at first base, he is probably dreadful at anything past it. I learned this the hard way. One man was not only the worst kisser in the world, he was so bad in bed it's fortunate he didn't put me off sex for life. Thankfully, he just put me off blonde men. I now exclusively date dark swarthy types because the experience was so unpleasant, although perhaps one day I will find a blonde Adonis to cure me of my phobia. Facebook-message me if you have Daniel Craig's cell phone number.

You may be an SG with the ability to separate sex from emotion, in which case, go play. If you prefer your sex spiced with a little meaning, though, that should be celebrated, too. It seems to be a biological fact of life that there are fewer guys than dolls of this persuasion. My girlfriends and I cannot have sex without feelings getting involved, no matter how hard we try, which may mean we'll inevitably have to depend on other methods of satisfaction at times (after all, masturbation is the thinking (wo)man's television set). If a man is unable to bring himself to call us his girlfriend, we are simply unable to shag him without it all ending in tears, and they are never his waterworks that get exercised.

Old stereotypes do, to an extent, die hard, so if you want to keep the power when you're dating a Distraction, don't have sex with him until he's right where you want him. All my PBs confirm that the act itself always makes the difference. Once you have slept with someone, you can never go back, and men, unless their minds are already hooked on you, may not want to go forward. One of the aforementioned eligible bachelors only makes a second pass at a girl if she wouldn't go all the way with him the first time. He freely admits that if she had already succumbed, why bother?

Some PBs of mine think it's a marvelous idea to have f★★k buddies. These are girls they have "no strings attached" sex with to alleviate physical frustration. As an SG, you are well within your rights to have a lover whose sole purpose is to relieve any sexual pangs you might have. That said, I haven't found an SG who feels this arrangement has worked for her, although naturally, I have several PBs who feel otherwise. Whatever the case, these males accept that their f★★k buddies are not platonic girlfriends. Sounds obvious, but to have a real platonic relationship, you shouldn't be "kissing" each other. If you suspect that hormones might take over in a PB's company, it may be necessary to maintain distance, or always have someone else with you in his presence for a little while, just to make sure there is no heat of the moment you both could get carried away in.

The reason I have so many PBs is that we have not exchanged so much as an Eskimo kiss. If you think you may want to get naked with them, you must accept that once those boundaries are passed, your relationship will never be the same. An exception—though it's by no means a guaranteed exception—is if you "accidentally" make out once with someone in a light-hearted manner. However, a "light-hearted" make-out session should be no more than a 10-second snog, maybe no tongues, and definitely frivolous. A longer smooch and it is liable to spell trouble. I was at a cocktail party holding court with three gay men when we discovered we had all kissed the same man, and we all still consider this lucky so-and-so a PB.

Bisexuality is probably something we should all contemplate more carefully, since the SG is all about keeping her options open. Several female friends have tried and enjoyed "kissing" girls. One sexually ambiguous SG reports that it is always sensible for your first experiences to be with someone who knows what they are doing. She now organizes visits to all-girl parties for her more curious SG friends.

There is a distinct possibility that since you spend most of your time at work, you may get involved with someone from there. It is inevitable that all your other co-workers will immediately find out.

Try to keep your behavior as discriminating as possible, so you can at least function in your professional capacity. This means no naughty nookie on site. One friend, after a moment of passion with one of her male trainees, had left her distinctive diamante encrusted stocking hold-ups over the back of a director's chair. Said director discovered them at the beginning of a breakfast meeting in the boardroom. This was not her finest hour. Fortunately, no one could take any serious action against her. My friend had made it her business to know precisely how many of the directors, almost all of whom were married, were "kissing" their PAs. As touched on earlier, please try not to get entangled with attached people. SGs who have affairs with the boss and married men give us all a bad name. This makes managing our worlds all the harder, as it just adds fuel to the fire of attached women's wary perception of us.

If you're dating someone "exclusively," when is it the right time to have sex? General SG consensus, garnered scientifically by selecting a focus group of females and feeding them vodka while playing Madonna's greatest hits, point to the third date rule as a realistic scenario. The fifth date was also presented as an option, but this was seen as being positively virginal. Standard methods to prevent clothes removal before outing three is to limit your alcohol intake, the time spent alone with him at yours/his, and not to get a bikini wax or shave your legs. However, I am aware of one SG who has been known to shave her legs mid-date to get round this.

When you're having sex, don't get hung up about what you perceive to be your body's shortcomings. Not only will he probably not have noticed before you draw attention to them, but such anxiety is not alluring to a man. Your Object will also be too busy worrying about his performance to be concerned with your slightly squishy belly. Your trump card is that you have breasts. They excite and fascinate men, because they don't have them (if your Distraction does, either diet or ditch him). And if you're over thirty, don't fear cellulite or wrinkles. Many attractive men of my acquaintance find the older woman far sexier than her younger counterparts; they know what they are doing in the bedroom and have fewer inhibitions. So allow your age to bring confidence into your own skin. This attitude will always be attractive to men, *thank God*.

Undoubtedly the older you are, the less shocked you'll be if some sexual boundary pushing is proposed. You'll probably find the prospect so tantalizing that you bring it up yourself. Of course, you have to remain within some sort of comfort zone, but there are always varying degrees of naughtiness that you can compromise on. One friend's Distraction loved the idea of handcuffs; the metal variety did nothing for her, but pink fluffy ones were an orgasmic compromise. Make sure you keep hold of the key, though; one SG friend lost hers while indulging in some solo action (don't ask), and her roommate had to help her out of her predicament. Fortunately her female roommate found her, as her male roommate would probably have asked to join in.

Some men are massively turned on by anal sex, which no doubt explains their frequent fetish for French women, who are apparently much more open to the idea. If you aren't, suggest other routes. You into him, for instance. He will either run a mile and not bring the topic up again, or you get a pain-free solution.

People are prone to finding the most extraordinary things a turn-on, so don't be afraid of talking through your fantasies. They are probably quite pedestrian and quite possibly shared by others.

Accidental Sex

Boys have one-night stands. Girls have Accidental Sex (AS). AS is when an SG gets involved in a situation that she rarely intended to go as far as it did, or believes such a liaison is going to happen only once.

Do not beat yourself up or feel guilty about AS. You wanted to do it at the time, you had fun (hopefully), so let it go. Almost every SG has done the same at some point, even if they won't admit it. Safe sex is advisable, but it doesn't always happen. Since you're a grown up, get thee to a pharmacist or doctor and deal with it, even if you are suffering from the hangover from hell.

Relationships rarely tend to come out of AS encounters. Therefore try not to mess up and have AS with someone you really like. I know it's hard, but irritatingly, if you're a boy it's all about the chase. Once you have AS with him, he's already won the prize. Invariably, the only way he will want a repeat performance with you is if you convince yourself that he will never return and move on. If a man sees you functioning fabulously without him, his interest may be piqued again.

In the long term, AS with someone you never have to see again is far easier to deal with than with someone you do, although there is potential for major misjudgement this way. One SG awoke to find a very attractive, but anxious, man in her bed. When she asked him what the problem was, he said he needed his medication. For multiple personality disorder. It took two PBs and her GBF's shiatsu (the GBF unhelpfully got scared so went and waited for them in the nearest cocktail lounge) to eject him just as his second personality declared squatter's rights. I jest not.

AS is more likely to be with someone you know, invariably a co-worker or PB. If it is the former, never, ever, have an exchange regarding the AS at work. You do not want to run the risk of being overheard or having a missive forwarded, damaging your career. Keep your poise around him at all times so a mutual respect can return between you both. If the AS is with a PB, unless both of you suddenly realize that you want to try and make an official go of things, you messed up. It will take months to get back on track, if ever. Sorry.

If you managed to be somewhat sensible and the interlude took place at your abode, usher him out by noisily getting ready for work. He should get the message as soon as the scent of toothpaste hits him. In the circumstances you didn't entice him back to your bed (accidents do happen) and you awaken from an AS situation, hung over, under someone else's duvet, aim for either the extremely early getaway or mid-morning departure, when there are less people about. If you have enough money on you, call a taxi; just don't expense it to work; otherwise it will be discussed in detail at the Office Christmas Party.

Sunrise is not as flattering as sunset. There will not be much you can do about your Panda Eyes if you wake in the Distraction's abode and he has no female roommates. However, if you have to get through a day at the office or a family get-together without having been home, you will just have to improvise. Jump in his shower, utilize any of his bathroom products you can, and deal with any major mascara issues by using his Vaseline and a tissue. The latter items will be located somewhere near his bed; best not to ask why. Our 24/7 culture is also there to come to the aid of the SG in her hour of unkempt need, with Duane Reade open all hours, and The GAP open most of them. One

SG who was having a playing-hard phase kept a spare top in her desk at work in case of any emergencies. If anyone else saw it, she claimed that it was there because she lived in fear of spilling something down her shirt. She's such a messy eater it was believable.

If you are hoping beyond all reason that your Object will contact you after your AS and he does not already have your number, you need to give it to him. A subtler option is to pretend you can't find your cell and ask him to call it from his phone so yours rings. Lo and behold, he has your number, and you his, but again, make sure you leave it to him to contact you. You must also expect that he probably won't.

The other, and hottest form of AS, is "ex-sex". Emotionally, it's almost always a head f★★k of the highest order, although physically there is nothing so blissful or so naughty as rediscovering the body of someone you used to date—and probably should be nowhere near. You know each other's sexual buttons, and the frisson of "kissing" someone you thought you never would again is almost always mind-blowing. Unless they were useless in bed to begin with; then it's just a useful reminder of why you are no longer with him. Numerous SG friends have ex-sex stories, but nothing tops the situation one sexually empowered SG friend of mine found herself in. Her ex had been on morning television as an "expert" on some subject. She was watching him while in bed with another ex. Both of them were involved in a begging war to have her back. The main reason for their desire was her determination to keep both of them ex's. Being an SG made her happier than being with either of them, an important thing to remember as we turn to the last chapter of our SG celebration.

DISTRACTION MANAGEMENT PART 2

Survival Tips

- A date is many things but it is not: a meet-up where he brings his friends, or Accidental Sex between 10PM to 3AM. Give up and find another fish if it's either.
- If you're unsure about your date, make it a pre-6 p.m. meeting.
- Consult friends to help you construct a suitable CL for date location and Object.
- Full kissing and cuddling is not the best plan until after Date Three.

CHAPTER 9

Survival of the SG Fittest

*I*N THE EARLY encounters of dating and "kissing," any relationship with a Distraction will likely be an ambiguous
one, where neither of you will be entirely sure of where you
stand. However, there will come a moment when either you
or your Distraction get so dissatisfied by the vague situation that
some definition will be required. The time has come when you
either regain official full-blown SG status or lose it to become an
Attached Girl (AG).

Many of us tend to be averse to direct confrontation in such matters close to the heart. Typically, the female is anxious to avoid accusations of getting ahead of herself, while the male will only reluctantly admit to being tamed. So if you suffer a sudden bout of shyness about baring your soul despite having already bared it all, it may be that it is actually a third party who clarifies it all.

I once attended a soirée with an Object when someone asked him, in my presence, if I was his girlfriend. He appeared aghast, but being a well brought-up boy he mumbled that, yes, I was, "absolutely," while his appearance morphed into that of a trapped mouse. This made me instantly steel myself against the inevitable, which came later that night when Mickey officially ditched me. There are of course other ways to end this story. Many an SG I know has discovered that she was someone's girlfriend because he introduced her as such. Sometimes the surprise has even been a pleasant one.

In an ideal world, if you find yourself falling for your Distraction, he should be shouting the news from the rooftops. Yet in this commitment-free, easy-refund world, my SG friends and I have found that for an increasing number of men, actually granting the title "girlfriend" is a huge deal. You may find that the Distraction requires a little nudging/management to make your status official. A reliable tactic so many of my AG friends have used is to turn on the serious charm with their Object's family and friends. Tread cautiously, though, with the males, so that your efforts aren't misconstrued as flirting. Do well with his nearest and dearest, they'll decide you're "a good thing," and start referring to you as his girlfriend anyway. If everyone around your Distraction has accorded you the title and you've already met his parents (usual drill: appropriate dress, CL, etc.), he's likely just to go along with it.

Either way, the ambiguous relationship ends in one of two outcomes: ditching or commitment. If it's ditching, there's similarly no gray area—"mutual decision" is a term perpetuated by Hollywood publicists whose Pinocchio-esque grasp of the truth is no doubt responsible for LA's nose job rate. The SG faces facts. You're either the ditcher or the ditchee.

• THE DITCH •

Ditcher

If your relationship is particularly ambiguous and you wish to just let it die a natural death, you may not need to take any direct action at all. If you can just gently drift out of "kissing" each other, rather than cause unnecessary embarrassment on either side, do so. Keep in mind that boys have a tendency to think about the ramifications of romantic encounters rather less than girls, so they may not rate the relationship as much as you do anyway. Several PBs of mine have been dumped by girls they did not realize they were going out with, much to their bemusement and amusement, so there may well be a good chance that no action need be taken.

This is the only time it's acceptable to ditch someone by using the silent treatment. Otherwise act your age rather than your shoe size and tell the truth. The love of my life's last words to me were "see you soon." He never contacted me again, or returned any of my attempts to get in touch with him. His behavior was the catalyst for my nervous breakdown. There was obviously something special enough for you to be with your Distraction to begin with. Give him the respect he deserves and end it properly.

A word of warning before you do the deed. Fools rush in to a relationship, but they also rush out. It is only natural if you sometimes have panic attacks about whether you want to have a boyfriend at all. After perfecting the art of the SG party, you must now learn the AG art of the compromise. Being an AG is not necessarily worse, just different; if you are having doubts, don't run from him in haste. Whatever your distaste over his unsavory habits, they may not necessarily be directly ditchable offenses . . . unless he does them in front of your mother.

There are times when it's vital you jettison your attachment. A friend of mine was working in a high-pressure job in a television newsroom where the computer systems kept going down on a regular basis. She made friends with the IT guy, who was actually fairly normal looking, and didn't resemble your stereotypical tech geek. At first, the relationship was fantastic. She had never been with someone who was so sensitive and who seemed to understand her so well. When she needed him to be attentive, he was. When she required him to take a step back, he did. Her friends loved him because he remembered their names and their backgrounds. Mr. IT was so in tune with Newsroom Girl that she soon realized it was because he was reading her e-mail. This is stalking. If a man's behavior to you—or indeed yours to him—ever degenerates into the realm of sneaking a peek at a phone to read text messages, or checking the call register, showing him or yourself the virtual door is probably the only option.

If you ditch someone, mind your manners. No need to sink as low as those litmus tests of disagreeable taste, Britney and KFed, and declare divorce by text. E-mail is slightly less dreadful, but a phone or even a face-to-face conversation is preferable and most proper. Gently explain that you had a great time but it's not working for you, and get out. Sometimes the Distraction might refuse to accept the concept that you just do not want to be with him and will keep attempting to remain in your world. If he resorts to ridiculous levels, you may need to be mildly impolite, but there is no need to be exceptionally rude and just ignore him. He is human, after all, and will eventually get the message, even if it is by accident rather than design. One SG friend dumped a man who just wouldn't take no for an answer and was so inundated with presents, flowers, and balloons that she started to distribute his gifts among her friends. Irritatingly I was late on the uptake, and all that was left by the time I got to her goodies was a dolphin-shaped balloon. I was subsequently spotted by the ex giving Flipper to a young boy at a bus stop because the child found it so hilarious. On registering the ex's stricken face, I informed my SG friend she probably wouldn't be hearing from him again. She never did.

 ## *Ditchee*

Rejection is never easy. We all have to deal with being rebuffed at some point; however, there are certain things you can do if you're the one being ditched to make the experience less painful.

Once he's told you it's over, whether it's in person or on the phone, quietly accept what he has said, then do your best to leave so you can keep as much of your self-respect as possible. If it's by e-mail, wait at least twenty-four hours and get your friends to check your reply before you send it. We've all been guilty of saying things in the heat of the moment that rarely look good in the cold light of day. One friend had a hissy fit at a restaurant and tipped a glass of wine over her partner before storming out, only to have to creep back in to a round of applause from their fellow diners to beg him for her keys. Furious about the red wine stain on his adored vintage army jacket and his humiliation in front of a maître d' he'd spent years tipping for special service, the man dropped them into her soup and walked out. She was left with the bill and never heard from him again. "Bunny boiler" behavior is never endearing.

After you've retreated to a safe zone, immediately allocate him the same ring/message tone on your cell as all other previous disappointments—the **Promise Much, Deliver Little (PMDL)** boys. The PMDLs are scoundrels who bruise egos or even break hearts and as such deserve the most ridiculous noise option your phone has to offer (ducks quacking, for instance). Now, if he ever gets in touch, your ringing cell phone will send you into tears of mirth rather than despair. Edit his name in your phone to a good reason not to contact him. For example, you could rename him "I'm bad news" or "Prick." Be careful, though, when implementing this. A particularly organized SG friend of mine synchronised all her cell phone contacts with her e-mail ones, and then sent out an automatically generated e-mail to everyone in her address book asking the recipients to check their details. Unfortunately, this meant that "Small Penis" and her other PMDLs all saw the nicknames she'd given them. Not perhaps her most magical moment.

For the sake of your sanity, you must not place him on a pedestal of perfection. His absence should not be allowed to make your heart grow fonder. Even though you were convinced it was a match made in heaven, heaven's decided it's not. There is no point daydreaming endless scenarios where he tracks you down to Best Buy and declares his undying love among a cluster of video cameras so the incident is relayed on all the television sets in the vicinity in climatic Nora Ephron rom-com fashion. Anything other than ex-sex rarely works, and that only lasts as long as the orgasm(s).

If an Object splits up with you, try not to hit the Internet or harass mutual friends to find out what and who he is up to. If the opportunity arises, refrain from checking his e-mail or cell phone. A man with a touch of the playboy about him was in the process of ditching a close friend of mine. He regularly checked his e-mail from her home computer and often forgot to logout, and once, in desperate state, she stole a sly glance at it. This was a mistake. She could have done without knowing the specifics of his porn order or the several SGs of her acquaintance bemoaning their AS with him. It also proved to be a fashion disaster for her. She found eye contact with these girls and him awkward, so for several months she was forced to wear huge bug-eyed shades, earning her the unfortunate nickname "Bono."

There will always be something positive you can take from the experience. Call it **EXploitation**. My friends and I now have a running joke that we take from each ex a "use" that will stay with us for years to come. The more inane the use, the greater the entertainment value for us all. One man shifted my TV 20 degrees to the right, which has enhanced my viewing pleasure every time I switch it on. An SG friend took this a step further and actually groomed her unfaithful boyfriend for his use before they split. He had a touch of the Gordon Ramsays about him, so she got him to teach her how to make the most delicious chocolate fondant puddings (one with runny, warm, gooey chocolate inside).

Implement, as much as you can, a policy whereby you try never to fall out with an ex. I do have one Genuine Girlfriend who has the sophisticated method of only dating people from a certain London area, miles from her abode, thus limiting the likely chance of seeing her exes to when she is visiting her new man for sex. She isn't normal, though, so for the rest of us, we're liable to run into them from time to time. It is not easy if you are single and the ex is with someone new, but an occupational hazard of being out is that you will bump into him. After all, out is where you probably met. A friend of mine wisely says the only time it's acceptable to run into an ex-boyfriend is when you are in a black-tie-affair dress and on the arm of a better-looking and more visibly successful man. Ideally, he'll be in sweaty sweatpants. Unfortunately, Murphy's Law dictates that it's more likely you who'll be colliding into him returning from *your* workout (this has happened to me). Does it really matter? They will have perfect recall of you in more compromising positions and because you are a happy SG, you are completely in tune with your body beautiful. And wearing very cute gym gear.

With determination, you will find a balanced state of mind about love affairs gone awry. There is a reason why you aren't together, whether it's his blindness to how incredible you are, timing, distance...Whatever the reason, don't let him make you hide yourself away. One of my SG friends, when dealing with a relationship gone wrong, tries to take whatever lessons she can learn from it. Then she moves on. She looks at her situation like pressing the "reset" button on a computer game. You get to start a new game and, with what you have learned, will hopefully fare better on the next attempt . . . while scoring more frequently.

• COMMITMENT •

Actually having a boyfriend is a massive culture shock for the SG. You're going from being slightly selfish to somewhat selfless, which can be a gigantic leap. If you are entering a relationship, remember your SG feistiness is what attracted him to you in the first place. Any unreasonable behavior on his part should be swiftly countered. If he demands you have that Brazilian, you can insist he has a back wax. Fair's fair in love and ingrown hairs.

You know that being an SG can be fabulously fun, but so can being with someone, if it works. Men are wonderful when the situation is right, but the unhappiness they can bring also knows no bounds. Make sure this is not you.

How do you manage a long-term boyfriend, to truly nurture and maintain a relationship? That is another book: for now, let's raise our glasses one last time in celebration of the SG.

SURVIVAL OF THE SG FITTEST

- Always keep in mind that you can be lonelier as an AG in the wrong relationship than you ever can be as an SG.
- If ditching, do as you'd be done to.
- If ditched, move your contact to the PMDL section of your cell phone—and your life. You're briefly allowed to go Big Duvet, but must then put yourself In Harm's Way of Play again.
- EXploitation—allocate him a use, the more inane the better.

The End?

S̶O YOU'RE SINGLE? **Your** life has only just begun. You're keeping your options open until worthy ones come along. This is the right decision to take. Men, rather than women, are much more likely to be single. If you want a Distraction, the odds are in your favor. Today's world has bequeathed to the SG the gift of time, which is finally on your side, so panic not. The average age of brides and mothers is ever increasing, society realizing that it is healthier to have fulfilled, confident women rocking and ruling the cradle and the world.

There is no right or wrong path, as SGs who have blazed a trail for us have shown. You have the choice to opt for the Madonna route of marrying a toy boy late in life, or the Elizabeth I one, avoiding matrimony altogether, instead courting and trailing admirers in your wake. Enjoy the fruits of these SG icons' pioneering. There's nothing to fear about being single. Instead, it is a life that can be celebrated with friends, family, and fabulous footwear. Indulge yourself. Be comfortable within your own skin and with your own company. The people in your world will appreciate the happiness radiating from you; it'll be infectious.

A single girl is undoubtedly in possession of a good fortune, as she has the freedom to lead the life she wants. All it takes is a little management.

ACKNOWLEDGEMENTS

——— ———

*T*HE ROAD TO publishing a book is a long, winding, and sometimes rocky one, and I would like to take this opportunity to
say a massive thank you to all my family and friends for helping me
along it (I *would* keep hindering my progress by refusing to remove
those four-inch heels).

I would also like to say thank you to the teams at Summersdale and
Skyhorse for all their support, in particular Stewart Ferris and Brando
Skyhorse. In addition, thank you to Jane Reilly and Faye Rogaski for
their tireless work on the book's behalf, Veronica Palmieri and Salma
Conway for their fabulous SG illustrations, and Sam Hiyate for his
North American perspective. Anthony Pye-Jeary, Tom Littlechild,
and everyone at Dewynters have kindly designed the most amazing
Web site.

The Single Girl's Survival Guide would never have been written
without some very specific help, and I am indebted to: Ele Clow and
the Queen's girls; Darryl Samaraweera; Daniel Bee (the best publi-
cist in the world); Wyckoff and his other two angels, Cat and Zoe;
Fin; Goli; his Bobness; Wheeler for his semantics; Amanda Johnson;
Charlie 'Slashie' Roberts . . . and LG for sharing his encyclopaedic
knowledge on the female species. I would have been lost without the

wise words of Caroline Turner, Lucinda, Jess, H, Yael, Diane, Josh, Frances, Julie, Peter, Louise, and Theo.

I would not have got here without the encouragement to continue writing over the years from some truly special people in the literary world: Ed Victor; Lizzy Kremer; Marjory Chapman; Toby Eady; Peter James; and Robert Huntington. Thank you so much for making sure I hung on in there, and I do so hope to work with you on future projects.

Words cannot express my gratitude to Mummy, Daddy, Nick, and Mads.

Alex and Frankie, you are not forgotten.